Laughing On The Way To Heaven

By Don Waddell

PRESS

Laughing On The Way To Heaven
A (mostly) humorous look at life from a Biblical perspective
by Don Waddell

Printed in the United States of America

ISBN 9781622300952

www.xulonpress.com

Foreword

Thanks for reading my book. Writing a book was not something I set out to do in the beginning, but after writing for the Southeast Christian Church newspaper, the *Outlook*, for 16 years, I have compiled these articles at the urging of many friends who blessed me with their encouraging words.

The articles are in no particular order and do not tell a coherent story together. Separately, however, I hope they provide some spiritual insights and glimpses of God at work in the lives of His followers. I also hope you are amused at my foibles and other Christians' misadventures that are often, well, just plain funny.

Special thanks to the *Outlook* staff over the years. I've worn out a bunch of editors.

Special, special thanks to the ladies in my life who provide inspiration and support:

Nancy, my wife and friend for over half a century.

Doris Waddell, my mom and constant encourager.

Emily Engelhardt, a devoted assistant who tolerated me longer than anyone else in my 45 years of professional service.

Laura Williams, world-class proofreader

Finally, I am eternally indebted to my good friend and boss Bob Russell who, over the past 46 years, had much to do with my growth as a follower of Christ.

Introduction

By Bob Russell
Retired Senior Minister,
Southeast Christian Church
Louisville, Kentucky

2 Timothy 2:15 Be diligent to present yourself
approved to God, a worker who does not need to be
ashamed, rightly dividing the word of truth.

I am honored to write the introduction to Don Waddell's book because he's one of the most fascinating people I know. He's one of those rare individuals who, the more you know about them the more impressed you are. God has placed Don in my path several times since we first met in 1966 when I came to Louisville to be the senior minister at a new church called Southeast Christian. I was a recent graduate of Cincinnati Bible College; Don was a junior at the University of Louisville.

Don had been an excellent athlete in high school, playing football and running track. He was also president of the Student Council, suggesting a bright future in the area of leadership. We played softball together on the church team, and Don also sang in the choir and attended Sunday School.

Don comes from a wonderful family. Don, his brother Steve and his parents were charter members at Southeast in 1962. Both Don's dad, Don Jr. and his mother, Doris, were faithful, core leaders serving in many church ministries, including finance, facilities and the library.

I officiated Don's wedding when he married Nancy Smith from Boston, Kentucky in 1967. Don reminds me from time to time that that was the wedding where I instructed him to "put the ring on the third hand of the left finger." He never was very good at following instructions, but the marriage has lasted for 45 years at last count. Don and Nancy have three children, Don the 4th, David, and Dawn; and four grandkids, Don the 5th, Devin, Erin and Amy. Nancy has been contending with Multiple Sclerosis since she was 19 and still raised their kids, travelled around the world many times and supported Don's career.

Don was drafted into the military just after graduation from the University of Louisville and went on to serve as a fighter pilot for 28 years, retiring as a full Colonel in 1995. He enjoyed a wonderful career serving his country and garnered many awards and decorations. Notably, Don flew 151 combat missions in Vietnam in 1971-1972 and compiled over 2800 flying hours in his career. He served in the Pentagon in the early 80s and was commander of Lindsey Air Station, Wiesbaden, Germany from 1991-1993.

We met from time to time while Don was stationed in various locations around the world. My wife, Judy, and I along with two friends, Doc and Jane Summay, stayed with Don and Nancy in Germany while we were on the way to and from Kenya. They were gracious hosts, showing us a good deal of the German culture during our brief stay.

Throughout much of his career, Don was active in churches all over the world, serving as an elder in several congregations. His first love was teaching, and Don has taught Sunday School for over 40 years in various churches at home and abroad.

In 1994, it was time for Don to retire from the Air Force after 28 years. He and Nancy had purchased a retirement home in Fort Walton Beach, Florida and planned to live out their retirement dreams near the beach and their boys and the grandkids who lived just two hours away in Tallahassee.

Good plan, we think, but God had other plans. Don and Nancy were visiting his parents in Louisville and attended Southeast one Sunday morning when they were so moved by the Holy Spirit that they decided to sell their retirement home and return to Louisville to be part of the work the Lord was doing at Southeast. Don is a great example of a Christian who elects to serve God in the ministry after retiring from a successful career.

Don joined our staff in August 1995 as Director of Facilities, a new position we desperately needed to get ourselves better organized. The church had been growing so fast we needed someone like a former military base commander to oversee the rapidly growing facility. Don did this job well, until we moved into our most recent building in 1998.

Recognizing his splendid spiritual gifts of teaching and administration, we transferred Don into the New Member ministry when we moved into our new building. As expected he excelled. Ultimately he became the teacher of two Sunday School classes that both were over 100 in attendance, and he was a popular teacher for many different classes and venues.

I was pleased to officiate over his ordination into the ministry in 2005, an event that made his wife Nancy especially proud. While she attended Milligan College, Nancy aspired to be a minister's wife but ended up married to a fighter pilot until she got her wish when Don was ordained.

In 2006, when I prepared to retire after 40 years at Southeast, I knew I was going to need someone to assist me in administration and scheduling. My former assistant, Barbara Dabney was Nancy Waddell's cousin, who was married to another Southeast charter member and our good friend, Bob Dabney. Barbara was quick to suggest that Don would be an excellent choice to be my assistant, but I wasn't sure a former Air Force fighter pilot and wing commander would agree to serve in this capacity. I also wasn't sure that Don would want to leave Southeast at that time. It says a lot about Don's loyalty and work ethic that he agreed to work for me and on staff as the New Member minister at Southeast.

As my assistant, Don has provided indispensable assistance organizing Bob Russell Ministries, coordinating my schedule, conducting monthly retreats for young ministers and generally doing all the things that I don't want to do. Meanwhile he continued to write for the *Outlook*, Southeast's excellent weekly newspaper. As you will soon discover when you dig into this book, Don is an excellent writer who brings wit and wisdom to the columns he writes. At the urging of many people, Don has compiled about 70 of the over 400 *Outlook* columns and published them in this book.

Now let me share a few things about Don that will help you better understand his columns just in case you don't know him personally. First, he is short. Some have said that is the reason I hired him--to make me look taller. That's not true. He's also bald. Last thing you need to know is that Don has a dog named Zacchaeus, a wimpy little, white curly haired pure bred mutt. Like his Bible namesake, Zac is a wee little man, and Don's Sunday School class reminds Don that Zac's owner is also a wee little man.

Don is a five-talent guy and as hard a worker as I have ever known. But more importantly, Don loves the Lord and is committed to giving his best to the Master, and I see his passion to share his faith and help others grow as disciples increasing the older he gets.

When I think of Don in light of Scripture, my mind goes to 2 Timothy 2 where Paul admonishes Timothy to "be strong in the grace that is in Christ Jesus...endure hardship as a good soldier of Jesus Christ." Paul speaks of a hard working farmer and an athlete who competes according to the rules. That's the Don Waddell I know, and I think you are going to enjoy getting to know him better in the following pages where he will look at life from a Biblical and humorous perspective.

TABLE OF CONTENTS

Foreword v

Introduction vii

A buffoon for Christ..17

I'll have a Blackberry with my oatmeal...........................21

I'm a 65-year old adolescent..24

Bet on number six in the last race 28

Any day that starts with a prostate exam... 31

Turning 55 and I'm not talking about a speed limit..........35

I don't mind fasting, it's the hunger that I object to..........39

I'm not a workaholic, I just love to work all the time.......42

Honey, our credit card company called today...................46

"I used to smoke, I used to drink...".................................49

Old age: Don't complain, proclaim...................................52

How do you say "thanks"
    to a guy who saved your life? 55

We don't use the "s" word in our family 59

My height is not one of my shortcomings 63

I wonder how Eliab arranged his hair 67

"Quick clean the house. The maid is coming!" 70

Romance in the hospital waiting room 73

"What's in a name? A duck by any other name..." 77

A regular spiritual exercise program will help you live
    longer, a lot longer 81

Men, surprise your wife. Do something thoughtful for
    Valentine's Day 84
Any landing you can walk away from is a good
    one...and other myths 87
May he rest in peace, right after his ex beats
    up his other ex 93
Husband lost on aisle nine 96
If there's such a thing as "Hurry Sickness,"
    I'm terminally ill 100
The theology of bumper stickers............................104
Once a proud Colonel, I'm now just a Holy gofer..........108
Odd that applying for Medicare
    would make me sick..111
Nancy's MS..114
My MS diagnosis. I didn't know it was spread
    that way 118
Shopping at the speed of light can be hazardous
    to your wealth 121
Sacrificial giving without the sacrifice....................125
My most expensive Valentine's Day ever 128
I have the eyes of an eagle but................................132
House cleaning tips for slobs 136
Returning to Vietnam 30 years later: Two granddads
    compare "war stories".....................................140
Barney Fife goes to the weight room 146
2,678 sermons without a fatality 150
My annual trip to pediatric "purgatory"...................154
Men being men; it's a scary thing to watch 158
57 is a good number if you're a steak sauce 162
If you're playing golf after you die,
    you're not in Heaven..166
Caring for aging parents...170
America is great because America is good 174
At least Job didn't have to worry about
    complete electrical failure................................178

For poorer, for poorer...182
To increase the romance, stay out of the hot tub..............186
Our hyperactive, hypoallergenic, hyper allergenic,
    hypochondriac dog..189
Life as a granddad is difficult...193
It is not good for man to live alone...he might
    hurt himself 197
Zac on steroids: Move over Hulk Hogan 201
If God's your co-pilot, change seats 205
Our Florida vacation: Heaven except for
    the tropical storm 208
There ought to be a law against grandpa
    abandonment..213
Black Friday at Toys R Us and other mental
    disorders...217
The traumatic Thanksgiving in Tallahassee 220
Caution: Reading warning labels can be hazardous
    to your health 224
My worst Christmas...228
Who said eight hours of sleep is "normal?"...................232
There's gold in them thar hills...or at least some
    glittering rocks (in my head)....................................236
Remodeling our "croak house".......................................239
Fishing for men is far better than fishing for fish............242
Teaching English as an evangelistic exercise 246
Would you choose your pet over your partner? 250
How's your spiritual diet?..253
That's the second unmanly thing you've done 256
Were there toys in the manger on Christmas Day?..........259
Valentine's Day shopping at Cracker Barrel
    can be very expensive 263
DNR for the dog?...266
Dinners for Eight, minus the hostess 270

A Buffoon for Christ

I am such a buffoon. In one of my weekly *Outlook* columns a careful reader (actually numerous careful readers) corrected me, pointing out that the computer in 2001: A Space Odyssey was named Hal, not Bob. Then in a subsequent column I noted that it was Jimmy Jones who sang "I couldn't sleep at all last night" in the 1950s. A more studious reader, Mark, gently reminded me that it was, in fact, Bobby Lewis who sang "Tossin' and Turnin" in 1961.

I hate to make mistakes, but you'd think after a mistake-prone 60+ years, I'd be used to it. Nancy tried to console me, "everybody makes mistakes" she said. Yeah, but not everyone puts their mistakes in black and white for tens of thousands of Pharisaical readers to dissect. Just kidding Mark. I appreciate the feedback.

As I celebrated my 65th birthday, I was reminded of some of my more memorable blunders. Crashing an otherwise perfectly good F-4 fighter-bomber while trying to land in a thunderstorm in Vietnam headed the list. Throwing a surprise birthday party for my mom's 80th birthday a year and three months early also made the top 10. But one of the most memorable gaffs took place not long after I joined the Southeast staff as the Director of Facilities.

I hadn't been on the staff long, but long enough to know that they needed help---more discipline, more rules and regulations. Just what a retired "Full Bird Colonel" could give them.

It had come to my attention that some obscure regulation mandated annual fire extinguisher training, so I informed my boss that I needed to demonstrate the proper use of the fire extinguisher to the assembled staff. Of course most of the attendees had little interest in fire extinguisher operation and generally busied themselves with inconsequential activities like preparing for Sunday worship, studying the Bible, leading people to Christ, and that sort of thing.

I knew that this demonstration had to go well or I would be the brunt of jokes until Christ returned. As the day of the staff meeting approached, I planned to rehearse the demonstration just to make sure that nothing would go wrong. So that morning I went to work early to practice. I broke the seal, pulled the pin and squeezed the handle to activate the extinguisher. It worked gloriously as a dense cloud of white power mushroomed in the air. This is going to be a very impressive demonstration, I thought to myself.

I had planned to embellish the demonstration a bit to heighten the dramatic effect. I had my lovely assistant dress in a white robe to protect her from the ensuing blast of fire suppressant. She was going to hold a lighted candle that I would extinguish with the white powder.

When it was my turn in the program, I went up on the chapel stage, confident in myself and my carefully rehearsed procedures. I calmly explained the reason we all needed to be able to operate a fire extinguisher: Lives would be saved, building damage minimized, world hunger abolished. If I'd been alive in 1871, the Chicago fire would have no doubt been prevented. Then I carefully went through the procedures to break the seal on the handle (noting that I had already broken it earlier during rehearsal). I pointed the fire extinguisher nozzle at the candle and then squeezed the handle.

Nothing happened.

I squeezed again, this time harder until my knuckles turned white.

There was no whoosh, not a speck of fire suppressant emanated from the nozzle. The candle continued to flicker, mocking me with its flame. I prayed for Christ to return... now!

It was very quiet in the chapel. Then our Worship Leader Greg Allen, who delights in needling me said, "Great demonstration, Colonel" and the place erupted with laughter. Greg was pretty sure even Jesus would laugh at my antics when we met face to face in heaven. I can just see Jesus slapping his knee and saying, "Well, Don the good news is that you won't need a fire extinguisher up here." Hardy Har Har.

What a buffoon. I later discovered that the pressure had leaked from the cylinder after my practice session before staff meeting...just as the instruction manual warned, if only I had read it.

Here are some lessons I learned about being a buffoon, just in case you've made a mistake or two in your life.

1. The only people who make mistakes are those who actually do things. Don't back off when you mess up.
2. Admit the goof up and move on. Learn to laugh at yourself. In fact, most people don't pay as much attention to your missteps as you think they do. Get over it.
3. If you mess up, you're in pretty good company. The Bible is full of some pretty extraordinary screw-ups. Abraham lied, Jacob stole his brother's birthright, the greatest Empire on earth crumbled under Solomon's leadership. In the New Testament, Peter denied Jesus and Paul persecuted Christians. Paul even described himself as "a fool for Christ." In his case, however,

Paul didn't mean that he was divinely mistake prone, but rather he would be happy for people to think him a fool for boldly proclaiming his faith in Christ.

Not wanting to put myself in the same class as Paul, the "fool for Christ," I now aspire to be a "buffoon for Christ." And that's what much of this book is about: my missteps in life and ministry, learning how to contend with day-to-day challenges, and my often faltering endeavor to become a fully devoted follower of Christ. I hope you'll be encouraged by my travails and less self-conscious when you fail to measure up to a Godly standard.

I particularly hope you'll be challenged, as I have been recently, to grow in my faith, and be less concerned about appearing foolish when I speak up for Christ or mess up along the way...or when I have to demonstrate the use of a fire extinguisher in front the church staff.

I'll have a Blackberry with my oatmeal

My good friend Zack Coblens met me for breakfast some time ago at Cracker Barrel. As is my custom, I was early and was passing the time checking my email on my Blackberry when Zack arrived and chided me for being immersed in my gadget. He was right, of course, since I am often consumed with my device when I should be interacting with others, sharing the Gospel, or figuring out how I'm going to pay for my rapidly increasing wireless bill.

I challenged Zack with the reality that in today's fast paced world, PDAs are an accepted way of doing business and nearly everyone has one. To prove my point, I elicited the opinion of our waitress. "Do you have a Blackberry?" I inquired hoping she would respond affirmatively. "Oh, yes!" she responded enthusiastically to my delight. I winked smugly at Zack just in time for our waitress to say "Do you want the blackberries on your pancakes or oatmeal?"

Sometime later I traded my Blackberry in for an iPhone in my quest to find the perfect communication device and was enthralled with all the apps (applications) that were available. I'm pretty sure I could become so consumed with these apps that I could avoid human contact entirely. One of

21

the apps is called Dragon Dictation, and it does a pretty good job of listening to the spoken word and then transcribing it into printed text which can then be saved or sent to some special someone via email or text message.

Since I do a good deal of writing (such as Outlook articles) this could come in handy I thought, and in fact some of this very article was transcribed on my iPhone. @;a&oimd. S-tys ##mloi*)jpme Cum sekt or whyu.

I was so excited with my new find that I rushed home to share it with my technologically challenged wife, Nancy. She readily concedes without apology that she is stuck in the 19th Century and has no intention of upgrading to a newer version of herself anytime soon. She thinks "a high tech message" is affixing a post-it to my iPhone. Like many Christians, she is hoping Christ will return before she has to learn how to reprogram the VCR to eliminate the annoying flashing "12:00" on the display. (My grandkids asked me recently, "Grandad, what's a VCR?)

Anyway, just before bedtime I announced that I wanted to demonstrate my newest technological acquisition. She feigned interest as I dictated a message that I knew would endear myself to her. I repeated slowly and distinctly into my iPhone, "I love Nancy Waddell, my wife and friend," and immediately sent the message out as an email to myself.

The wonderful love message to my wife went out at the speed of light and returned to my iPhone to demonstrate, not only my love for my bride of 43 years, but my technological acumen as well. Eager with anticipation I showed the message to my wife whose facial expression changed from curiosity to disbelief to amusement. My Dragon Dictation did a reasonably good, but not perfect, job of transcription. The message as transcribed was, "I love Nancy, what the hell, my wife and friend."

Needless to say Nancy didn't rush out the next day to buy an iPhone.

Nevertheless, I love technology, I really do. Of course the danger is that we become so infatuated with the means of communication that we forget the importance of the message, and this has direct applicability to Christians.

There's another app I have on my iPhone, and unlike my Dragon Dictation, it always gets the message right. I have a Bible on my iPhone, which allows me to look up Scripture, the very words of God, at the speed of light. But in 1439 when Gutenberg invented the printing press, the ordinary Bible printed on paper was high tech, and I'm sure some 15th Century geeks marveled at the printed words on a page and missed the message, the eternal, life changing, profound words of God, God's communication with us through the Holy Spirit and not electrons.

Writing in *Faith That Prevails*, Smith Wigglesworth, puts it this way: *"Never compare this Book with other books. Comparisons are dangerous. Never think or never say that this Book contains the Word of God. It is the Word of God. It is supernatural in origin, eternal in duration, inexpressible in value, infinite in scope, regenerative in power, infallible in authority, universal in interest, personal in application, inspired in totality. Read it through. Write it down. Pray it in. Work it out. And then pass it on."*

Pass it on by any means possible: Blackberry, iPhone, Dragon Dictation, word of mouth or better yet by your actions...which may include putting down your high tech device and sharing God's message of hope with someone close to you.

I'm a 65-year-old adolescent

Arriving at church early one Friday morning, I was greeted by a twenty-something young lady who smiled cheerily and said, "Hey, you look cool!" I think she meant that as a compliment, but I was feeling self-conscious in my blue jeans, shirt hanging out, wearing loafers and no socks. I toted a sporty backpack similar to the one my 15-year-old grandson carries and wore wraparound sunglasses that I found at the beach the previous summer.

There was a time in my military career when I might have been court-martialed for wearing such apparel in public. There was a time as a teen I would have been grounded for about a decade for going to church in such sloppy attire. There was a time as a church employee, Bob Russell (our senior minister at the time) would have sent me home to put on a tie and socks. But now, I'm cool.

I feel like a 65-year-old adolescent.

I can still hear my parents scolding me as a youth after some childish outburst: "Grow up" or "act your age." Back then they wanted me to act older than I was. Now that I have my Medicare card and have been recruited for membership in the AARP for 15 years, the expectation is for me to be less mature, at least as it pertains to my sartorial choices.

But after 28 years in USAF, I understand uniforms and dress standards.

For instance, in high school and college my uniform was "preppie" and consisted of blue oxford cloth shirt, khaki pants, Bucklehorn belt, Alder socks and Bass Weejuns, which my parents bought for the outrageous price of $12.99. My hair was combed into a "Princeton," and I was cool.

Later in the Air Force the UOD or "uniform of the day" was more institutionalized and for the most part I loved wearing a uniform. Not only did the girls swoon, but since I wore the same thing every day, I didn't have to make any major decisions before breakfast. I mean, I'd get up in the morning and say "well, I think I'll wear blue today." Now every morning is a perplexing ordeal, and I stare at the array of shirts and slacks in my clothes closet for what seems like hours trying to decide what to wear.

Compliance with uniform standards in the military was specific and detailed. For instance, all buttons needed to be buttoned, shoes spit shined, and shirts starched stiffer than a board. Most challenging was the worrisome "gig line." The "gig line" refers to the alignment of the shirt, belt buckle, and trouser fly. These must be lined up, plus or minus a millimeter or two. That's not exactly essential to national defense but pretty important to a new recruit in Basic Training. Curiously, today my gig line now has an unsightly lump in it that was absent during my younger, slimmer days.

Few issues around the church provoke more passionate debate than music played during worship and what we wear to church on Sunday. I know that is true with the crowd I hang with and for the most part I understand because many of us spent the majority of our lives putting on a coat and tie or a Sunday dress to go into God's house and worship. (A lady in my senior's Bible class claims to have incontrovertible evidence that Christ wore a tie when he went to the temple.) Still I have come to appreciate the position of our leaders in encouraging more and more casual attire at church. About this I would make two points:

1) What we wear to church (as long as it is modest) doesn't matter to God. Dress codes and styles are a human invention. I've diligently searched the Scriptures and can't find the commandment "Thou shall wear a tie on Sunday morning." I did find some pretty specific guidance if you are a Levite priest and then you'll look spiffy in your "breast-piece, an ephod, a robe, a woven tunic, a turban and a sash." I can see our current Senior Minister, Dave Stone preaching in his Ephod. Wouldn't that be special?

On the contrary, God makes it pretty clear that he doesn't care about what a person looks like. Consider 1 Samuel 16:7: But the LORD said to Samuel [concerning Eliab], "Do not consider his appearance or his height, for I have rejected him. The LORD does not look at the things man looks at. Man looks at the outward appearance, but the LORD looks at the heart."

2) We want everyone to feel comfortable when they come to church. I recall going to church in Hawaii some years ago where everyone was decked out in their "Sunday go to meeting" clothes which consisted of cutoffs, sleeveless shirts and flip flops. I would have felt pretty conspicuous had I donned my customary suit coat and tie. Younger folks with their more relaxed attire and the poor would feel similarly out of place if they visited Southeast and everyone was "dressed to the nines." We especially don't want to make young folks feel out of place since they are the future of the church.

I am pleased my church has no compulsory dress standards, and I love the variety of apparel considered appropriate. We don't have to worry about what so and so is wearing, but can accept everyone regardless of their circumstances or personal preferences. We want all to come to know Jesus as Lord and Savior even if they don't dress like our parents and even if they most resemble a 65-year-old adolescent.

Bet on number six in the last race

Bud Scheule died on April 27, 2003. For the 13 months leading up to his death, he had been my best friend, though we were about as different as two people could be. Bud was a large man while I am normally characterized as short. Bud was a former nightclub owner; I was a megachurch minister. Bud was an octogenarian; while I was a relatively youthful 57.

Bud described himself as the biggest bookie in Jefferson County in the 1960s, and he loved to bet on horse races. Bud taught me how to read a racing form and advised me how to bet on the ponies. "Take the long odds in a short field," "Bet on number six in the last race" was his counsel. All in all, Bud was not the type of guy a megachurch minister would normally hang with.

I first met Bud on March 15, 2002. Lisa Thompson, my secretary at the time, called me and related that she had talked to a prospective volunteer named Brenda Schuele whose 88-year old husband was dying of cancer and wasn't saved. Lisa told Brenda that she'd send me to visit with Bud and lead him to the Lord. She had a lot more confidence in my evangelistic skills than I did. Besides, I had a 2:00 tee time that afternoon, but I figured I could visit with Bud, lead him to the Lord and make it to the golf course in time to practice my putting.

So, I grabbed my Bible and pressed off to Prospect confident there'd soon be one more soul in God's Kingdom. Bud and I made polite conversation while Brenda prayed in the kitchen. After a while, I said to Bud: "I understand you want to give your life to Christ." "No" Bud responded with a wry smile, "actually I'm an agnostic and I'm pretty sure I can make an agnostic out of you too." His response surprised me...and aroused my competitive instincts.

I began a series of visits with Bud on Fridays. I called these visits, "Fridays with Bud," which sounded more like a beer commercial than an evangelistic endeavor. During our sixth visit, we chatted about world affairs, horse racing and reminisced until Bud said, quite unexpectedly: "I'm ready to give my life to Christ." I was startled but gathered my wits enough to review the plan of salvation and have him repeat the good confession. I was ecstatic at Bud's decision and Brenda and I pressed him on the subject of baptism, but he resisted.

Still, I met weekly with Bud, until, again quite unexpectedly, Bud called me at church one rainy Friday morning in May. "You all got enough water over there?" Since it had been raining for several days, I thought he was talking about the weather. "If I came over there this morning do you think I could get baptized?" "Absolutely," I shouted, finally getting it. With the help of several church staff members, Bud was helped into the baptistery where I baptized my best friend and the prayers of many of us were answered in dramatic fashion.

I continued my weekly visits. During one visit in December we prayed, and I went to leave but Bud held on to my hand. "You know it's amazing to me," he said "that it took me 89 years for me to meet my best friend." "You mean Jesus?" I asked. Bud smiled broadly and responded with a twinkle in his eye, "Oh yes, him too." I was honored to be considered Bud's best friend and thanked God for bringing us together.

From my experience with Bud, I learned that leading someone to Christ is a team effort. Bud's wife Brenda had arranged for us to get together and prayed incessantly. Lisa was sensitive to Brenda's situation and sent me on the mission. Southeast member Pat Butler visited Bud weekly and others took communion to him. My ABF class, the Cornerstone, sent cards of encouragement to Bud and prayed for him.

The funeral, orchestrated by the energetic and irrepressible Brenda, was a testimony to Bud's faith in Jesus Christ. Pictures and *Outlook* articles of Bud's baptism adorned the chapel and everyone who came to the funeral home heard the Gospel message from Brenda in one form or the other. I met many of Bud's friends, customers and coworkers of the past. Often the odor of alcohol was apparent. The most common comment was: "You mean Bud was a Christian?!" It occurred to me then that Bud had come to Christ late in life when his body was weakened by cancer, but in death he became an effective evangelist nevertheless.

The Saturday following Bud's funeral was Derby Day, the annual run for the roses that Bud followed closely during his bookmaking days. I'm not sure God works this way, but it seemed too coincidental that the winner of the Derby that year was Funny Cide...horse number six. But Bud didn't bet on Funny Cide. In the end, Bud bet on a sure thing. He gave his life to Christ, and now I look forward to an eternity of Fridays with Bud.

Any day that starts with a prostate exam...

A ny day that starts with a digital examination of your prostate can only get better. Now for my female readers I know you can't relate to this specifically, but you endure enough personal indignity at the doctor's office that I'm sure you can relate to my feelings.

The inspection of my unmentionable areas (or "uncomely parts" as they are referred to in the King James Version of the Bible) was part of my annual physical. Unlike many men, I am a real believer in annual trips to the doctor for a periodic inspection. I mean, most of us wouldn't miss a 50,000 mile checkup for our beloved automobile but getting our vitals check every 12 months is an anathema.

As an Air Force pilot, physicals were mandatory. Generally speaking when flying multimillion-dollar aircraft in the vicinity of large urban areas, the Air Force and FAA desire that pilots not have heart attacks, strokes or intestinal "disbarisms" (that's a USAF euphemism for flatulence, which can be very distracting when you're cruising around at Mach 1.3 or pulling 6-7 g's).

But I was even more conscious of the need for a periodic physical after returning from a "mission" trip to Alaska. (I know what you're thinking, but Eskimos need Jesus, too.) During our visit, I met Nathan, a gentleman not too much older than I am. His minister had had prostate cancer and taught a Bible study lesson on the Christian and health, encouraging his listeners to get periodic checkups. After this prompting Nathan made an appointment with his doctor and discovered cancer in his prostate. Immediate action was taken and Nathan recovered. Had he waited, he might not have lived.

So, I was greatly relieved to hear my doctor say, "Mr. Waddell, you have a clean bill of health." We love to hear the doctor say those words, don't we?...until the bill actually arrives in the mail.

All this led me to think about the "Great Physician." What would be my results of a spiritual examination? Doctors examine our hearts, lungs, blood and other organs to determine our physical condition. What would Jesus check? Here's what I think a spiritual check-up would consist of:

1. How much time do you spend in prayer? "Watch and pray so that you will not fall into temptation. The spirit is willing, but the body is weak." Mark 14:38. "Be joyful always; pray continually; give thanks in all circumstances, for this is God's will for you in Christ Jesus." 1 Thessalonians 5:16-18

2. How often do you read God's word? How much Scripture have you memorized? "But the one who received the seed that fell on good soil is the man who hears the word and understands it. He produces a crop, yielding a hundred, sixty or thirty times what was sown." Matthew 13:23 "Study to show thyself approved unto God, a workman that needeth not to be ashamed, rightly dividing the word of truth." 2 Timothy 2:15 (KJV)

3. How much time do you spend helping others? Matt 25:37 "Then the righteous will answer him, 'Lord, when did we see you hungry and feed you, or thirsty and give you

something to drink?'...40 "The King will reply, 'I tell you the truth, whatever you did for one of the least of these brothers of mine, you did for me.'"

4. How's your spiritual diet? Then Jesus declared, "I am the bread of life. He who comes to me will never go hungry, and he who believes in me will never be thirsty." John 6:36

5. How many people have you led to Christ? "Then Jesus came to them and said, 'All authority in heaven and on earth has been given to me. Therefore go and make disciples of all nations, baptizing them in the name of the Father and of the Son and of the Holy Spirit, and teaching them to obey everything I have commanded you.'" Matt 28:18-20

6. How much exercise do you get working for the Lord? While you can't work your way into Heaven, it is an indicator of your commitment to the Lord. "For we are God's workmanship, created in Christ Jesus to do good works, which God prepared in advance for us to do." Ephesians 2:10

7. What have you given up or sacrificed for Christ or for your fellow man? "Be imitators of God, therefore, as dearly loved children and live a life of love, just as Christ loved us and gave himself up for us as a fragrant offering and sacrifice to God." Ephesians 5:1-2

8. We can tell a lot about a person's physical health by testing various substances that come out of the body. You can also measure your spiritual health by examining what comes out of your mouth. "For out of the overflow of the heart the mouth speaks. The good man brings good things out of the good stored up in him, and the evil man brings evil things out of the evil stored up in him. But I tell you that men will have to give account on the Day of Judgment for every careless word they have spoken. For by your words you will be acquitted, and by your words you will be condemned." Matt 12:34-37

It's comforting to hear a physician pronounce that we are healthy, but that diagnosis doesn't guarantee us much at all. Because we are mortal, our health could go anytime. We could die physically, in innumerable ways. But when we stand before the Great Physician and He gives us a clean bill of health, that diagnosis will last for eternity.

Turning 55 and I'm not talking about a speed limit

When I come home after work Nancy usually has the mail stacked on the couch next to where I sit. All too often there is little of interest to me, just the usual junk mail, catalogs, overdue notices, and a *Cat Fancy* magazine. On this particular day, two magazines were all that were there for me to read.

One was *Modern Maturity*. It was addressed to me. If you are under the age of 50 you may not know that *Modern Maturity* is the magazine published by AARP. I recall the first issue I received many years ago; it was a significant emotional event in my life since only yesterday I was 18 (or so it seemed). One article featured on the front cover of *Modern Maturity* caught my attention. "From flab to fit in just 12 weeks." "What a joke," I thought to myself, "anyone eligible to receive this magazine might not have that long to live."

As I thumbed through the magazine, I eyed ad after ad for the geriatric minded. There were ads for Ensure, washable briefs, every conceivable motorized wheel chair, and Depends sold in quantity. I noted an article on seniors' attitudes on various social issues. Not too surprisingly they were not too keen on the subject of euthanasia, though support for mercy killing increased the lower the age group polled.

All this comes on the heels of my 55th birthday that I refused to celebrate this summer. I guess I'm in denial. I mean, 55 is a good number if you're a speed limit or a tree. 55 is a superb golf score, but as far as ages are concerned, it is the pits. Nancy tried to console me: "You're only as young as you feel." Reminded of the increasing aches and pains when I get out of the bed each morning, I thought to myself, "Egad! You mean I'm that old?"

Growing old is awful, and Nancy is no help in my attempt to preserve my youth. She describes me as the poster boy for Geritol, the darling of the menopause set, and the sex symbol for women who no longer care. I remember as a youth growing up with my parents, and reading the obituaries at the dinner table, a ritual I found rather morbid. Now I find myself glancing occasionally at the obituaries, just to check that my name isn't there.

I recall my mom or dad occasionally noting that someone about their age (mid 50s) had died. I thought to myself, "Dead at 52, that's not too bad. At least they lived a full life." Now I think the same thing about people who die at 95 or a hundred. Charter member and founding elder, the late Butch Dabney was fond of noting that he can't wait to get to heaven. According to him he had lived long enough then that he had more friends in heaven than on earth.

It is comforting to know that we are living longer. If I had been living at the turn of the century, I would have died 5 years ago. Now as the life expectancy exceeds 78 years I may have 23 more years or so. I got an email from a friend recently that outlined some advantages of getting old. He noted that: Your investment in health insurance is finally beginning to pay off. Kidnappers are not very interested in you. It's harder and harder for sexual harassment charges to stick. Your secrets are safe with your friends because they can't remember them either. Your supply of brain cells is finally down to a manageable size. You don't need the roof shingles with the 30-year warranty. In a hostage situation you are likely to be released first.

The Bible is very helpful in sorting out my mixed emotions about my advancing years. Consider what the Bible says about old age. First, it chronicles the lives of some pretty old people. We all know about Methuselah who lived to be 969 years old. His life insurance company must have made a lot of money on him collecting over 900 years of premiums before they had to pay off. (I wonder if he was a member of AARP.) Adam lived to be 930 years old. That's remarkable in its own right, but consider that he had other children besides Cain and Able when he was 800 years old. I don't know about Adam, but my kids wore me out. Can you imagine being 800 years old and changing diapers. Worse yet, think about dealing with teenagers after eight centuries of living. "Oh Dad, you just don't understand."

What else does the Bible teach about old age? The elderly are to be revered for their wisdom. "'Rise in the presence of the aged, show respect for the elderly and revere your God. I am the LORD." Leviticus 19:32 Or as Job said in chapter 12: "Is not wisdom found among the aged? Does not long life bring understanding?" I haven't noticed any additional reverence since I received my first copy of *Modern Maturity*, but since I came to work at Southeast I have learned to value the insights of those senior to me and am learning daily how much wisdom they possess if we "younger" folks will just listen. Also as I read the Scriptures, it is clear that the length of life is far less important than what we do with that life God has given us.

I am in awe of Southeast's senior adults. These men and women are an active, contributing part of the wonderful ministry here. They are a big part of the church volunteer pool, and I don't know what we'd do without them. At a time of life when many are content to become disconnected, sit idly in a rocker or lose themselves in "retirement living," these wonderful people are making a difference for their church, their Lord and themselves.

The final Biblical lesson is that no matter how many days God gives you on this earth, whether a person lives to be a hundred or their life is cut short in middle age, we are to live our lives to God's glory. "And whatever you do," Paul writes "whether in word or deed, do it all in the name of the Lord Jesus, giving thanks to God the Father through him." Colossians 3:17

I don't mind fasting, it's the hunger that I object to

Fasting is a fundamental Christian practice. It is mentioned 33 times in the Bible, it was a common Old Testament discipline, and Jesus fasted 40 days before his temptation. Now, let me ask a question. When was the last time you heard a sermon on the subject of fasting?

You'll hear a hundred sermons on eschatology, a thousand on tithing or how many angels you can stack on the head of a pin before a preacher will suggest a Christian forego his or her staple of donuts, fried chicken or baked beans.

Fasting is not a popular topic in the evangelical circles. Why is that? I have a theory. Given that we are so holy (not really), eating is our only vice (or some would have us think). We "Bible thumpers" do love to eat, and most Christians think fasting is something akin to not going back for thirds at the monthly church potluck.

Actually, I don't mind not eating; it's just the hunger I object to.

I have to admit that I haven't had extensive experience fasting. My first experience with fasting was kind of a dare. For over 30 years we have supported World Vision, an organization that allows you to "adopt" a child overseas and help feed him or her through monthly contributions. In 1979, while stationed in Holland we were challenged by a World Vision representative to go a day without food to develop an appreciation of what it's like to be hungry.

We agreed to do this as a family and decided to start at midnight. The next day our collective stomachs were growling in unison by noon and by dinnertime we were reduced to watching the minutes tick by slowly. At midnight there was a line forming at the refrigerator and we ate until it hurt. All in all I think this was a great exercise that taught us a lot about how the majority of the world's population feels most of the time---hungry.

In 1998, my boss at the time, the late Brett DeYoung, was teaching about fasting in his Weekend Group class and was fasting himself as a consequence. He taught me about fasting for spiritual reasons and introduced me to the practice of fasting to enhance my prayer time and closeness to God. This is why you most commonly hear the word "prayer" used in conjunction with fasting, as in "prayer <u>and</u> fasting."

Actually, my favorite fast involves giving up cumquats and eggplant, and I can endure this fast for quite a long time. (Remember I'm a minister at a megachurch so I have to be mega-spiritual, too. Not!) I have also been known to don sackcloth and ashes just to accentuate how much I am suffering.

The point of fasting, according to *Holman's Bible Dictionary*, is to lay aside food for a period of time when the believer is seeking to know God in a deeper experience. "It is to be done as an act before God in the privacy of one's own pursuit of God." e.g. Exodus 34:28. I guess the sackcloth and ashes thing kind of defeats the purpose.

I have found that at significant times in my life fasting has been very helpful. Yet, I'm still a beginner. Normally I conduct a sunset-to-sunset fast, not eating after dinner until dinner the next day. This is not too rigorous and essentially amounts to missing breakfast and lunch. At the same time when coupled with increased prayer, achieves the intended purpose. Again the sackcloth is left in the closet and the ashes in the dust bin.

My longest fast was just over two days. I have known people who have gone a week without solid food, and I understand that one minister in Louisville goes on a 30-day fast every year. For longer fasts, returning to eating solid food requires self-control and patience. Generally, gorging yourself on hotdogs and nachos after a long fast is not a good idea. You need to return to eating slowly. Matter of fact, that is where we got the word "breakfast," as in break [your] fast.

Recently my good friend and Oldham Pastor Kurt Sauder introduced me to another kind of fast, a media fast. He suggested I try going without TV or radio for a period of time. I fell in love with this routine. Not only did I have more time for Bible study and prayer, but I felt much better without the usual allotment of tragedy, disaster and mayhem on TV or the shouting matches on talk radio.

Our first media fast really turned out well for Nancy and me. We did a lot of things we hadn't done for a while---like talk to each other. I learned her name was Nancy. She has four grandkids. We read a lot and I felt very productive. It also allowed me time to draw closer to God and to pray.

I don't think I'll ever become a world class "faster." But I do think fasting, whether from food or the media, is a helpful spiritual exercise. You might give it a try. My guess is that God will bless you for the experience, and you will be drawn closer to Him in the process.

I am not a workaholic, I just I love to work all the time

My wife, Nancy, calls me a workaholic, but I disagree. Workaholics are compulsive; they have to work. Me? I love to work, and I always have.

I'm not sure who wrote the caption for my high school yearbook photo but it reads "I'd rather be sick than idle." In that respect, I maintain that I inherited my penchant for work from my dad who was once described by a neighbor as "the 'workinest' man I ever saw."

I like the way the late Katherine Graham, publisher of *The Washington Post*, characterized those of us who are passionate about our work. She said words to the effect of: "To love what you do, and believe that it matters. What could be better?"

But I must admit that a lot of what I do is for personal fulfillment and that I can certainly overdo it. I don't think that is part of God's plan for my life. So, recently I had to agree with Nancy, I had been pushing it pretty hard at work and a little R&R was long overdue.

All this talk about a mini-vacation began with a simple comment my wife, Nancy, made in the presence of Family Minister Rusty Russell and his wife Kelly at a Focus on the Family event some years ago. Nancy observed that she appreciated Rusty's article in the *Outlook* about spending more time with his family.

She then said she wished I'd spend more time at home. From that simple comment came an impromptu three point sermon, which concluded that I needed to spend more time with Nancy and with me packing my bags and heading south toward the hills of Tennessee for some rest for my body and for some quality time with my bride.

On the way down, I was proud of myself. I made it 57 minutes before I checked my voice mail. I had also secreted my laptop and several hot projects into the car just so I'd have something to do while Nancy was sleeping. (Sleeping has always been way overrated in my mind.) As we entered Pigeon Forge, just outside of Gatlinburg, my plan for rest and relaxation began to unravel. Since our objective was rest, I was surprised when we stopped to shop at an outlet mall before we even got to the hotel, for heaven's sake!

It was supposed to be <u>my</u> vacation, <u>my</u> rest and <u>my</u> relaxation. Shopping is none of these to me. Worse yet, at this mall there were shops stretching as far as the eye could see but not a golf or computer store among them. "What are we doing here?" I questioned. Nancy said she was Christmas shopping...in March!?

When we shop I'm especially concerned about Nancy's health. "You don't look too good," I'll say. "Maybe we should go to the hotel room and get some rest." Or I'll whine, "I'm not having fun anymore."

After making a purchase at the 17th shop, I was a nervous wreck. I was certain I'd have to find a part time job now just to pay for this 3-day get away. Not only that, but I felt like Nancy's pack mule carrying the packages and moving the car as she navigated resolutely from store to store. This is not restful. When we finally did check in to the hotel we were in the room about 15 seconds when Nancy said, "Let's go downtown." Guess what downtown Gatlinburg consists of?...thousands of shops, stretching as far as the eye can see and not a golf or computer store among them.

By the time my R&R was over, I was exhausted and felt like I needed to go back to work to get some rest. Counseling the spiritually impoverished, teaching lessons on eschatology and saving souls is certainly less tiring than trying to keep up with Nancy at an outlet mall or shopping till we drop in downtown Gatlinburg.

However, I must admit that getting the proper amount of R&R is a Biblical concept. God modeled how we should live our lives when He rested on the seventh day after creating the world. He made it more explicit in the Pentateuch (the first five books of the Bible) when he told the Hebrew nation to "Remember the Sabbath and keep it holy."

Unfortunately, the Pharisees took this simple admonition to its absurd extreme and allowed absolutely no work on the Sabbath. They went as far as defining how many steps you could take on a Sabbath's Day journey, surmising that about half a mile was permissible. Jesus set us free from the minute observance of the Sabbath, but made it clear that we are to live balanced lives without being either lazy or over worked.

More than anything else, it is the example of Jesus that causes me to critically examine my life. He had three years to change the world, yet he lived an unhurried life. He got away with his disciples often to rest and relax. He always had time for people and prayer. It seemed he welcomed interruptions to his routine when it meant he could help someone in need.

Our challenge today is striking a balance between working hard in a way that will honor God (Col. 3:23-24), leaving time and energy for friends and loved ones, and getting the proper amount of rest and relaxation. That is particularly difficult in today's 24/7 world of speed-of-light emails, ubiquitous cell phones and jobs that can consume us and rob us of our joy, our health and our relationships. God made us for Himself and for each other. He did not make us for the rat race. Periodic breaks for rest and relaxation is a virtue clearly supported by Scripture, but spending large portions of my R&R at an outlet mall is not.

Honey, our credit card company called today

Last month Dave Stone, our senior minister, preached a sermon on debt and challenged us to be completely debt free in seven years. I think I can do that mainly because at my age it's likely I'll be dead in seven years, all those insurance policies will pay off, my kids will inherit it all and I'll be debt free.

Well maybe that's not exactly what Dave had in mind, but I appreciated his insights for my younger friends and associates, because debt is something Nancy and I have struggled with for most of our married life. Matter of fact, after many years of being significantly in debt, Nancy and I are finally in pretty good shape financially. Praise God. Of course, our current situation is enhanced by the kids being on their own, me having three jobs, Social Security and an Air Force pension. It's also improved since we have gotten our credit card debt under control. But it wasn't always that way.

I remember when Nancy had all her credit cards stolen. I was sharing that tragedy with my mother and she said, "Well, you called all companies and had your credit cards cancelled, right?" "No," I said matter-of-factly. Incredulous, mom said "why not?" "Simple," I responded, "the thief was spending less than Nancy was."

This is an old joke but it's very appropriate to an incident that occurred at our house not long ago. You know any conversation that begins with "Honey, our credit card company called today," is not going to end well. That's the way a recent chat with Nancy began on a Saturday morning just after she had returned from Canton, Ohio where she had been enshrined in the Visa Card "Hall of Fame." Just kidding.

Nancy said she was quizzed by the credit card company representative who was calling because of the unusually large number of recent purchases that aroused their suspicions. But as Nancy reviewed the conversation in which the credit card representative rattled off purchase after purchase at department stores and women's boutiques around the city, I began to feel like I had been robbed...by my own wife.

In her defense, Nancy told me she had met a friend who attends our Weekend Group at the mall, but I naively assumed they had met for a Bible study or prayer walk or some such. Nancy failed to mention that her friend was a salesperson at one of the mall department stores. I noted that our walk-in closet was already crammed full of clothes. How could Nancy need another item of women's apparel?

"Everything was on sale," Nancy proclaimed proudly. "Think of all the money we saved." Unlike the U.S. Congress, I've never fully grasped the concept of saving by spending, but perhaps the economic course I took in college hadn't been taught from a politician's or compulsive shopper's point of view.

At this point, I was considering demanding Nancy surrender her credit cards. It was at that exact moment Nancy read the final entry from the credit card statement, "Computertown USA, $1765." Whoops. I had forgotten about that one. Nancy winked at me with that look wives have perfected since the first primordial mall opened. "Got ya!" she said triumphantly as I sunk down into my recliner defeated and speechless. I never saw it coming.

I suppose we're like most Americans. Little wonder the average family's credit card debt is $15,799. Little wonder the average family feels like both parents need to work to make ends meet. When we don't restrain ourselves, we get into trouble financially and eventually our credit card company or bank will call to become better acquainted. But, are we any happier because of all the stuff we buy? Apparently the answer is "no."

A Gallup poll found that the level of happiness was pretty consistent among people with incomes above $30,000. The report said in part: "Many people are under the illusion that the more money we make, the happier we'll be. We put all our resources into making money at the expense of our family and health. (But) we don't realize that our material wants increase with the amount of money we make."

In his book *The Progress Paradox* Greg Easterbrook had a similar conclusion. Easterbrook's carefully researched and heavily footnoted book found that while our standard of living has increased dramatically since World War 2, our level of happiness hasn't increased appreciably. By every indicator we are healthier and wealthier, but not happier.

As always the Bible has the answer on how to obtain true happiness, and it has nothing to do with credit cards. Jesus said in Matthew 6: 19-21 "Do not store up for yourselves treasures on earth, where moth and rust destroy, and where thieves break in and steal. But store up for yourselves treasures in heaven, where moth and rust do not destroy, and where thieves do not break in and steal. For where your treasure is, there your heart will be also."

"I used to smoke, I used to drink..."

—◆—

There was a song popular in the 1950's which began, "I used to smoke, I used to drink, I used to smoke, drink and do the hoochie goo." While I never figured out what the hoochie goo was and as far as I know never did it, I must confess that I did participate in the other two activities.

When I quit smoking at age 28, I didn't smoke or do the hoochie goo, but I would confess to imbibing more than occasionally. It's a fighter pilot sort of thing. Paul's counsel to Timothy to take a little wine for his stomach's sake (1 Timothy 5:23) was some comfort to me, but my wife kept prodding me, "How much wine does your stomach really need?" She was also correct that the Bible says nothing about martinis or scotch on the rocks.

Over the years as I rededicated my life to Christ, I drank less and less. Then when I was called into the ministry and joined the Southeast staff in 1995, I understood that I would have to quit consuming "adult beverages" altogether. You can look on this as a condition of employment, or just the right thing to do, but after much prayer I took my last drink of an alcoholic beverage on December 31, 1994, and I have never regretted that decision. After imbibing for over 30 years, I thought I couldn't live without it, but it has been easy, except that I developed a taste for beer that I have never lost.

A number of my minister friends enjoy a non-alcoholic brew, and I resisted that for quite a while feeling that if someone saw me in the restaurant with a glass of liquid containing a beer-like looking substance they wouldn't know if it contained C_2H_5OH molecules or not.

So, I established a personal policy that I would consume non-alcoholic beer only if I were outside the city limits. As far as I know this created only one incident. I had traveled to a church conference in Indianapolis and dutifully submitted my receipts with my travel voucher upon return without carefully reading them beforehand. The restaurant where we ate did not make a distinction between "beer" and "non-alcoholic beer" so I had some explaining to do when our pesky head of finance reviewed my request for reimbursement for a beer.

But about five years ago, I thought it would be OK if I purchased non-alcoholic beer at the grocery store and consumed it at home. So I nervously went to the store for a couple of items and nonchalantly waltzed by the beer cooler carefully looking out for an elder or perhaps our senior minister Dave Stone lurking in the shadows ready to pounce on me for pulling an item out of the cold beer section.

I discretely and quickly pulled out a six-pack of non-alcoholic brew and hid it beneath several other items in my cart and made my way to the checkout line. The express line was too long so I elected to use the self-checkout lane. I scanned my other items and reconnoitered the area again for elders and quickly scanned the non-alcoholic beer.

What a mistake. Bells literally sounded, lights flashed and the checkout screen projected a message in big, bold letters. "See the checkout manager before proceeding." Egad! This was awful. I was busted.

Apparently the machine at the store doesn't distinguish between beer and non-alcoholic beer and the alarm system was installed to prevent a teenager from making an unauthorized purchase. I cannot begin to describe my humiliation at being "carded" as a 60-year old at the grocery store for purchasing non-alcoholic beer. The clever clerk examined my driver's license looked at me and said, "yeah, you appear to be over 21." My response was "you don't know any elders at Southeast, do you?"

As I look back on my years as a consumer of adult beverages, there were certainly more embarrassing moments than uplifting ones, more harm resulted than good. This is consistent with our culture as a whole where lives are destroyed by alcoholism and families suffer from abuse associated with drinking. Now, binge and chronic drinking are becoming common among kids at younger and younger ages. This is not good.

Realizing this, the Southeast position paper on "Alcohol" concludes, "That is why we ask every Christian to consider becoming a total abstainer from alcohol. Alcohol can negatively affect your health, lower your inhibitions, and diminish your Christian witness. Abstaining from alcohol ensures that you will never become an alcoholic, and abstinence sets a positive example for your children and others."

Having been a teetotaler now for over 17 years I haven't missed drinking at all. I certainly don't miss the hangovers and occasional embarrassing situation most imbibers encounter along the way.

I like the way Paul phrases it in Ephesians 5:18: "Do not get drunk on wine, which leads to debauchery. Instead, be filled with the Spirit." I have discovered that the more I am filled with the Spirit, the less interested I am in spirits...even the non-alcoholic variety.

Old age: Don't complain, proclaim

It was the morning after except, as a teetotaler, there hadn't been an evening before, at least as far as I could remember, but then again at my age remembering isn't something I do very deftly anymore.

I didn't exactly roll out of bed. It wasn't a fall either. Actually I creaked out from between the sheets and lifted myself unsteadily on to the cold floor. Everything from the top of my bald head to my gout infested feet ached.

I made my way uncertainly to the bathroom where, thanks to a faulty prostate, I had been more than an occasional visitor the night before. Without my glasses I squinted to read the label on my pill bottle to make sure I was taking my arthritis medication and not a second dose of Geritol. It then took me several minutes to negotiate with my fingers to button my shirt.

I navigated uncertainly to the den and flopped down in my easy chair, exhausted from the ordeal of getting ready to go to work. I wasn't overly enthusiastic about going to work that day since once again I'd be stuck up at the church's retreat center for discipleship training with a bunch of post adolescents from the student ministry irreverently wearing blue jeans and flip flops, flaunting their iPhones, iPads and Apple computers, and threatening to change everything about my church that I hold dear.

I longed to sing Rock Of Ages again, all 17 verses. Wouldn't it be nice if the current worship music weren't played at the threshold of pain with drums and acoustics pounding in my ears? I pined for the return to simpler worship where the audience sat in pews, the preacher wore a tie, and the choir looked like they'd fit in well on the cover of *Modern Maturity* magazine.

That morning, I slumped further down in my easy chair discouraged by my travails. Now I was anxious to get to work so I could complain about my situation to anyone who would listen. Then I remembered that I had an *Outlook* article due. The editor wanted me to write about the joys of being a senior...or something along those lines. I couldn't remember exactly, but all I could think of is that we seniors have a lot to complain about.

Uncertain about what to say I remembered my mom celebrated her 88th birthday recently, and so I decided to ask her to share her thoughts on how she remained upbeat through the better part of her 9th decade on this earth.

I'm really proud of my mom, Doris Waddell. She was a charter member of Southeast, active in a weekend group, Women's Circle and long-time volunteer. She was our librarian at Southeast for many years and loved the facility and people she got to work with. Yet when the church leadership decided to demolish the library and erect in its place a coffee shop, she was disappointed but accepted the change as necessary to accommodate a younger demographic.

She dove into the information age many years ago, buying a computer when most seniors were still trying to figure out how to get the flashing "12:00" off their VCRs. She has a Kindle, pays her bills on line, and used the Internet and specialized software to research and publish a three-volume set of family genealogy.

But the thing I appreciate about mom is her positive outlook, even as a senior who has to contend with aches and pains and changes at church she often doesn't agree with. She always has positive things to say about friends and church, deftly avoiding the gossip-like conversations that sometime predominate at senior's gatherings.

From my chat with mom, here's what I concluded about how we can make the most out of our senior years and avoid becoming a grumpy, negative old fogey. I can reduce her guidance to one principle.

Even though we seniors seem to have a lot to complain about, don't complain. Nobody likes a whiner and worst of all it creates a negative attitude within you. Stay upbeat and positive. The Bible says: "A cheerful heart is good medicine, but a crushed spirit dries up the bones." Mom resolved long ago not to complain about the typical senior concerns when her kids, grandkids and friends came to visit. "Nobody likes a whiner," she said "and I want people to want to come see me."

As I listened to my mom, I thought of a nifty little saying that summarizes my thoughts now on aging and how to avoid the traditional pitfalls of negativity and complaining. "Don't complain; proclaim." By that I mean don't ever complain. It sours your disposition and it bores others. When you find your conversation turning negative, just stop it.

Rather than complaining, proclaim the Gospel, the good news of Jesus Christ. Thank God that while you may be enduring the pains of old age here on earth, you are that much closer to getting that new body and an eternal home with nothing to complain about forever.

Perhaps people will say about us what Moses wrote about Abraham in Genesis 25:8: "He took his last breath and died at a ripe old age, old and contented..."

How do you say "thanks" to a guy who saved your life?

L ast month I had lunch with Jeremy Urekew. Jeremy was the paramedic who responded to my 911 call on December 14 when I had a medical emergency following bone fusion surgery. To put it simply, Jeremy's quick and professional response to my 911 call saved my life.

Since this was the first time someone had saved my life, I was unsure how to properly express my appreciation. A thank you note seemed inadequate so I threw in a gift certificate to a nice restaurant and mailed it off. Sometime later, Jeremy and I talked on the phone, and he agreed to meet me for lunch since I was anxious to learn more about him and my medical situation.

While we ate, I asked how many calls he usually makes in a day, and he responded 4 or more. Then he said something incomprehensible to me. He said I was the first person to get back to him and express my appreciation in this way. I was dumbfounded. Of all the people who Jeremy had rescued, no one had taken the time to say "thanks?"!

Jeremy is a likeable, engaging young man who talked rapidly, his conversation occasionally interspersed with colorful language. His father is a college professor, and his mother was a paramedic. As a teenager, Jeremy rode along with his mom on an emergency run in which one of his friends was injured. That experience hooked him. He was destined to become a paramedic.

A self-described "adrenaline junky," Jeremy lives life to the fullest. Recreation includes rock climbing, rope rescue, kayaking, and ballroom dancing. When he's not working as a paramedic, he "relaxes" by working in the emergency room of a local hospital. The second job is necessitated by the low paramedic pay. I was stunned when Jeremy told me that he got paid $10.23 an hour. Are you kidding me? Not only are special skills required for the job, but it seems to me that savings lives should pay a salary comparable to doctor, nurse or plumber, never mind the outrageous salaries of professional athletes, Hollywood movie stars, or some such.

Since I was unconscious throughout most of my emergency situation, I asked Jeremy to fill in the blanks. I do recall that just after midnight on a cold December evening, after Nancy had gone to bed, I was watching TV when I suddenly felt an enormous pressure on my throat in the area I had had surgery on the day before. Almost immediately I began to have trouble breathing and called 911. I managed to say my name and address, and since the fire station is very close to our house, the fire trucks arrived within minutes. To my astonishment, the fireman didn't come inside so I went outside to get their attention.

Unable to talk now, I waved my hands and pointed at neck. It was frightening. I was becoming light-headed so I made my way back into the house, woke Nancy up, gave her the cellphone and laid down in the dining room and passed out.

Minutes before, Jeremy and his partner were awakened in the middle of the night and hustled (considerably faster than $10 an hour might prompt one to move) to their ambulance. They made it to my house in record time. Good thing, since I stopped breathing not long after they arrived.

Acting swiftly, Jeremy assessed the situation, assured my wife it was going to be OK, and put me in the ambulance. On the way to the hospital my heart rate dipped to 30, my eyes rolled back in my head and I nearly went into cardiac arrest before Jeremy inserted the breathing tube and restored my breathing. My throat was so swollen that he couldn't insert a normal sized breathing tube, but fortunately for me he had a pediatric tube, which was not normally carried in his ambulance.

All this took place while the ambulance rushed to the hospital, siren blaring. Jeremy turned me over to the Baptist East emergency room personnel and returned to get some rest. I went to ICU and began my 12 days of Christmas in the hospital.

I asked how my situation compared to others he had responded to. My situation was in the top three of his 10 years of experience, but not the most frustrating. He related one incident in his past where he had to carry a rather large woman down a flight of stairs.

On the way to the hospital, she was not breathing so he inserted an intubation tube into her mouth, but struggled due to the swelling in her throat and inadvertently broke two teeth in the process. She recovered but later sued him, despite the fact that his prompt, decisive actions saved her life. Are you kidding me?

I wasn't satisfied that a thank you note and gift certificate were adequate thanks for someone who had saved my life so I thought I'd probe into his relationship with Christ in case he needed a little "spiritual CPR." After all as a minister that's my calling, and I must confess I get paid a good deal more than $10.23 an hour to lead people to Christ.

To that end, I asked about church and his spiritual beliefs. Jeremy was candid and sincere in admitting that he was an atheist. I shared that I had a similar, skeptical Outlook as a young adult so I understood. At the same time, as I honestly sought to understand life and God and the meaning of life, my spiritual journey took me back to God.

How else do we understand the most important issues of life: Our origin (where did we come from), the meaning of life (without God it's meaningless), morality (what is right or wrong, how we should behave) and destiny (what happens when we die). The alternative to God is hopelessness and despair and living out our incredibly brief time on earth only to die and disappear into nothingness (the atheist's belief), or worse (Hell as revealed in the Bible).

I didn't persuade him to my way of thinking over lunch, but we have gone out to lunch several times since then. He even came to my Weekend Group (Sunday School) where I interviewed him about life and his spiritual beliefs. He's a good man. Matter of fact, given his considerable volunteer service to others I told the class that "Jeremy would make a darn good Christian, if he weren't an atheist."

I can't tell you how much I appreciate Jeremy. It was the heroic actions of Jeremy that saved my life. His professionalism and quick response allowed me to live and write this column. He saved my life; I'd love to be able to lead him to Christ who can save his life for eternity.

We don't use the "s" word in our family

I was waiting in the examination room to see my doctor for my annual physical. I had already spent 40 years in the "Wilderness" waiting room and had exhausted all the customary reading to pass the time: Old *Field and Stream* magazines, a *Time* magazine covering the inauguration of Jimmy Carter as president, and of course the dire warnings from drug companies of the possible catastrophic consequences if you use their product.

Then I noticed a rather large poster warning women of the dangers of Osteoporosis; it asked "Have you lost height?" I trembled at the thought. I've always been, well, short of stature, and I was aware that we often get shorter as we age, but I'd never had the nerve to check it out.

I glanced around the room. I was alone. There were no hidden cameras I could see (but course I guess if I could see the camera it wouldn't be hidden...but I digress), so I bravely mounted the scales, stretching my diminutive frame as much vertically as possible. At that point, I had a moral dilemma. Do I take off my shoes? "Ye shall know the truth and the truth will"...well probably confirm that I had been lying about my height all these years.

I had a flashback to 1957 before football season began. Clipboard in hand, my coach was taking my measurements as I stood on the scales. The device revealed that I was 5'5 ½ inches tall but he wrote down 5'7". We all knew that was a lie, but lived with the myth that the additional 1 ½ inches would instill such fear in our opponents that they probably wouldn't even show up for the game.

Anyway, back to 2011: I opened my eyes to see what the scales revealed...5'4 1/2" tall. Egad. I was shrinking faster than I thought. If I lived long enough I will totally disappear altogether.

I have been short all my life. Actually, I prefer the term "normal sized" which is what I encouraged my troops to call me when I was their commander and had the power to reduce them in rank or send them to jail. (We didn't use the "s" word on my base either.) I figured I was normal and everyone else had a growth hormone problem. In any event, I consider myself an authority on all short subjects, and I want to tell you it's the pits.

The disadvantages of being "normal sized" were carefully chronicled in a 20/20 TV program on short people I recall seeing many years ago. Many of my associates (I am avoiding the term "friend" here for a reason) asked me what I thought about the show. Actually, it went over my head. If you didn't see the show the ABC investigative reporter sought to answer the burning question, "Short men, does it really make a difference?" Their conclusion was yes, it does make a difference. Such is the stuff Pulitzer Prizes are given for?

The crack ABC team took a group of diminutive men, placed them in a line-up and had a group of women select the guy they'd rather date. Invariably the ladies selected the taller guys even when told that the shorter fellow was a millionaire, a best-selling author or an albino leprechaun who would grant her three wishes. The program went on to define short as less than 5'6" and asserted that being short, on average means that the individual will make $600 per year per inch <u>less</u> than their taller counterparts.

Now I know why the church pays me so little. My over-sized boss (6'5") at the time must have made a couple of mil a year. 20/20 also interviewed Robert Reich, the Clinton administration's 4'9" Secretary of Labor, who according to the $600 per inch formula must pay the government to work. Secretary Reich is short even by my standards. Matter of fact, Robert Reich is so short his family tree is a Bonsai, or so I have been told. The investigative reporter concluded in her report that bias against short people may be the "last form of discrimination." Perhaps she should have said, "the <u>lowest</u> form of discrimination."

What's the point of all this? I think there are at least two points to be made. One, we live in a society that is obsessed with physical appearance. We want our men tall, dark and handsome and our women blond and well built. Anyone not measuring up to the Hollywood standard is subject to ridicule or becomes the object of jokes. When physical appearance is the primary focus of our relationships is it any wonder why these relationships fail so often?

But this is not God's focus. In fact He couldn't care less about how we look. As I have noted before, when speaking of Eliab the Lord said: "Do not consider his appearance or his height, for I have rejected him. The Lord does not look at the things man looks at. Man looks at the outward appearance, but the Lord looks at the heart." 1 Samuel 16:7. As Christians we must be extremely careful not to evaluate others by their appearance.

Second, we shouldn't evaluate ourselves by appearance either. Many reduce their effectiveness for the Lord because of a poor self-image developed after years of comparing themselves to the Hollywood standard. You may have a dif-ficult time believing this but I have never thought of myself as short. Honest. The Lord and my parents gave me enough self-esteem that try as I may I have yet to convince myself that I am less capable than my taller counterparts.

I know I'm 65 inches tall (or at least I used to be) because it says so on my driver's license. But I don't feel 65 inches short. We need to look at ourselves as God sees us, a potential saint if we trust in Him completely. We need to honor God with our bodies. 1 Corinthians 6:19,20 "Do you not know that your body is a temple of the Holy Spirit, who is in you, whom you have received from God? You are not your own; you were bought at a price. Therefore honor God with your body"---whether it's short, tall, fat, or skinny.

My height is not one of my shortcomings

S ome time ago, Dave Stone preached a sermon on anger and told a story about him and his son, Sam, standing in line for an hour at an amusement park to ride a roller coaster only to be turned away at the last minute because Sam wasn't tall enough. Monday after the sermon I bumped into Dave our 6'4" senior minister in the atrium and joked that I had a similar experience at Kentucky Kingdom with my grandson, only I was the one who was too short.

Dave laughed politely and then asked sincerely but naively, "Really?"

Though I am a diminutive 64 and one-half inches tall, I've never considered my height to be one of my shortcomings. It's good to know that according to the current politically correct terminology, I am now just "vertically challenged" or "height impaired." For all these reasons, I consider myself an unimpeachable authority on short subjects, and I would make the point (in contrast to the ABC reporters cited previously) that there are many advantages to being short, or "normal sized" as I prefer to describe my stature.

First of all, while the science is inconclusive, there are studies that show that short people live longer. I think that's because we breathe denser air. My personal observation is that as a statistical group, normal sized people are more intelligent than their taller counterparts. You see all those cells that go to make up a 6'4" body come at the expense of brain cells (nothing personal Dave!).

Other advantages include: When I go to a basketball game people almost never yell "down in front" at me, I don't have to reach as far to tie my shoes as my taller counterparts, and, best of all, sometimes I get into movies for half price.

When I was a colonel and a vice commander in Germany, my boss, a crusty old two-star general was always bragging on me. At staff meeting one day all the senior officers were assembled and he put his arm around me and said, "This Colonel Waddell is a model officer." My chest swelled with pride until I returned to my office and looked up the definition of the word model and discovered that it is "an undersized, non-functioning replica of the real thing."

I remember my experience in Air Force survival training. After several hours of mock escape and evasion, we were captured and "tortured" by Air Force personnel, masquerading as enemy soldiers whose job it was to break us "Yankee American air-pirates." One of the torture procedures was to cram us into a very small cage, so small a normal sized person couldn't move at all in the hours they were encaged. I delighted in frustrating my captors by turning around so my rear end greeted them when they opened my cage. I paid for this disrespectful maneuver, but it was worth it.

Nevertheless, I must confess that I've worried a lot about my height in the past. To compensate, I tried an Afro hair cut in college. That got me an extra six inches or so. It also got me a lot of peculiar looks from my African-American friends. Now I've lost my hair so that won't work. Other normal sized people have tried more extreme measures. One San Francisco police candidate was a half-inch short of the 5'8" height requirement to become a police officer. He beat himself in the head with a 2 by 4 until the calluses and swelling allowed him to make the minimum requirement.

The Bible has a couple of things to say about being short. You have to read it pretty closely to discover the real truth, but Bob Russell (a guy I look up to...but not too much) and I agree that it is sound Biblical doctrine that short is better. Bob cited Knee-high-miah, the Old Testament governor who orchestrated the rebuilding of Jerusalem.

I offer for you the example of Saul and David. When the Children of Israel asked for a king they got Saul, "an impressive young man without equal among the Israelites---a head taller than any of the others." 1 Samuel 9:2. Well, we know what happened; Saul didn't work out. I guess we could say he fell short. His replacement, King David, was a "normal sized" person who became the best king ever. This led the Lord to reveal a profound truth, one apparently lost on today's women...short is better.

The New Testament is not silent on the issue of size. After years of exhaustive research I have found incontrovertible evidence that Christ was, in fact, 5'3" tall. Really. Believe it or not, the December 2002 issue of *Popular Mechanics* did a study on "The Real Face of Jesus" and based on forensic science found that Jesus was just over five feet tall.

The Bible holds up Zacchaeus, a "wee little man was he," as a positive example. On a more sobering note however, the Bible reminds us in Matthew 6 that we can't add even a cubit to our height by worrying. A cubit?? That's 18 inches! I'd be happy with an extra quarter cubit or two.

Most important, we need to recognize that our physical bodies are just a temporary home anyway. As a Christian we are guaranteed a new and better body when we die. 1 Corinthians 15:42*ff* "So will it be with the resurrection of the dead. The body that is sown is perishable, it is raised imperishable; it is sown in dishonor, it is raised in glory; it is sown in weakness, it is raised in power; it is sown a natural body, it is raised a spiritual body."

In short, I am happy with my earthly, economy-sized body. But I'm looking forward to a new and better one in the not too distant future, and when I get to Heaven I want to be able to dunk the basketball. I plan to stand tall on my first day in heaven, look Dave Stone squarely in the eye and say, "I'm not doing anything for the next 100 years shorty, want to play some basketball?"

I wonder how Eliab arranged his hair?

I was waiting for my Weekend Group to begin when my good friend Susan Metts approached and asked casually if I drew the illustrations that often accompany my *Outlook* articles. "No, Mike Stewart does those drawings," I replied "why do you ask?" "Because the caricature of you has too much hair," she replied matter-of-factly. And this is what I get from my friends!

My mind immediately raced to 2 Kings chapter 2, verses 23 and 24. "From there Elisha went up to Bethel. As he was walking along the road, some boys came out of the town and jeered at him. 'Get out of here, baldy!' they said. 'Get out of here, baldy!' He turned around, looked at them and called down a curse on them in the name of the Lord. Then two bears came out of the woods and mauled forty-two of the boys."

To be honest, I'm not at all sensitive about my lack of hair and actually like its practicality. I recall an experience some years ago when I was getting dressed with three others in the men's locker room after my workout. One guy stood before the mirror to fix his hair. He took with him a large bottle containing a blue, gel-like substance that looked for all the world like a bottle of slime, absent the icky green color. He spent several minutes preening, carefully pulling his hair into a multitude of small peaks. When finished, he looked like a combination of Pee-wee Herman and a person who just grabbed a live high voltage electrical wire.

Another person looking not unlike former Vice Presidential candidate John Edwards, began running his fingers through his rather long hair trying to get the majority of his follicles heading in the proper direction. He then grabbed a pistol-like blow dryer and began grooming in earnest for what seemed like 15 minutes, after which he stood back to admire his coiffure.

Finally another locker room user decided to tend to his hair or absence of hair in this case. This follically-challenged man took out an electric razor and shaved his head. Granted it didn't take as long as the blow dryer guy, but it seemed like a long time nevertheless.

I thought to myself, "Man, these guys are really vain." When it was my time to tend to my hair, I took the palm of my hand, placed it on the nape of my neck and moved my hand forward in a single motion to my forehead. I was done and ready to greet the world.

I remember when I was vain about my hair. Of course, it is easier to be vain about your hair when you actually have some. In my hirsute history I have had a variety of "dos." As a young lad I sported a burr. In junior high, my mom insisted I wear a flattop, replete with Butch Wax. Would that be hair for an heir? In high school, while JFK was president many of us elected the "Princeton" styling, and I held tenaciously to this style long after JFK had gone and long after I lost the most important prerequisite for this coiffure...hair.

I began losing my hair at an early age, and the receding hairline that made me look mature as a young adult made me look, well...old as I advanced in age. Worse than that, the less hair I had, the longer it took me to arrange it into something that resembled a Princeton. Like many aging men, I tried the infamous comb-over for several years but tired of the time consuming task of combing two or three strands of six-foot long hairs in concentric circles over my male pattern baldness.

Almost 10 years ago, after wasting countless hours in front of a mirror trying to recapture the look of a teenager circa 1963, I gave up on my vanity and decided it was time to quit worrying about my hair. I bought a pair of hair clippers and found a new hair stylist, my wife, Nancy, and returned to the burr style of my youth.

It was a big step for me and I worried that people would be shocked at the change. I anticipated people gawking and whispering behind my back about my new look with comments like: "He looks so old;" "he looks so distinguished;" or more to Susan's point "he looks so <u>bald</u>." In fact, no one seemed to care about the length of my hair, aside from an occasional bald joke before my Sunday School cronies.

Looking back on the experience, perhaps I was more vain than I thought; maybe as vain as my locker room companions.

I remembered Eliab who was the handsome contender to become the first King of Israel. Despite his good looks, the Bible teaches that he was not selected, reminding us of the truth that God doesn't care what we look like and we shouldn't either.

"But the LORD said to Samuel, "Do not consider his appearance or his height, for I have rejected him. The LORD does not look at the things man looks at. Man looks at the outward appearance, but the LORD looks at the heart." 1 Samuel 16:7

I wonder how Eliab arranged his hair?

"Quick, clean the house. The maid is coming!"

"**D**on!!" Nancy cried with a perturbed tone in her voice that always takes me back to the time I was a child, and my mother was sending me to stand in the corner. "Get off the couch and help me clean the house. The maid is coming tomorrow." I was puzzled, as I always am, at this conundrum. "Isn't that why the maid is coming," I asked incredulously, "To clean the house?" "Oh, silly," she said again with that parental tone and then she rattled off a list of duties for me that made the likelihood of me finishing the ESPN Wales-Scotland snooker match very remote.

Housework is one of my least favorite activities, ranking right up there with Chinese water torture and herding cats. But cleaning up before the maid comes is an imponderable. It's kind of like washing the dishes before you put them in the dishwasher, which is another routine practice at our home.

Of course I understand why Nancy goes through these machinations. Since Nancy is afflicted with Multiple Sclerosis she needs help with the housework, and I realize that if we tidy up first the maid can concentrate on the more difficult, odious tasks. Still, it seems incongruous to clean the house before the maid comes to clean the house, if you know what I mean.

Women are funny about houses being clean. Generally, if a man can find the remote, and the couch is accessible amid the discarded newspapers and empty fast food bags on the floor, he's happy. But a woman isn't satisfied unless brain surgery can be safely performed in the guest bathroom. Nancy is normally neurotic about these things, but she goes off the deep end when my parents come over. It's even worse when friends come by.

Rich and Pam were considering buying a patio home similar to ours, and I invited them over to look at ours. When I got home from work, I casually mentioned that they might be coming over later that evening. You would have thought I said the President and First Lady were coming for dinner. Nancy began to bark out restrictions: "They can't go upstairs it's a mess, can't go in laundry room there are too many dirty clothes, can't go in master bed room, can't go in garage."

"Can we show them the walk in closet?" I asked just to needle her a bit. A look of horror swept over her face. Our "walk in closet" is something of a misnomer. It's more a "climb over or burrow in closet" with all the clothes piled in heaps and a collection of women's shoes that would shame Imelda Marcos.

"OK," I said sarcastically, "when Rich and Pam come over I'll just have them stand on the front porch, and I'll describe the house to them." When I picked myself up off the floor, I got the vacuum out and began cleaning the living room.

When it comes to housework, the job I hate the most is changing sheets. Nancy insists that we change them every week just when I'm getting them broken in and comfortable. I figure you need to change sheets when they get so slippery from body grease that you slide out of bed in the morning. I really think changing them once a month or even every other month is overkill.

Changing sheets is a complicated job, too. Periodically we have to flip the mattress so Nancy's side doesn't become permanently dented. (It is an understatement to say that she sleeps a bit more than I do.) Then we have to put on the mattress cover that is about 17 sizes too small for the mattress and takes a "Body by Jake" type guy to stretch across the mattress. After my muscle cramps subside from the stretching ordeal, we put on the fitted sheet. We always struggle to figure out which way this rectangular shaped sheet should go and normally have to try several times before we get it right. (Often we need marriage counseling when we're done.) Afterwards there is the other sheet that we sleep under and then two light blankets and then the main covers. For reason I can't begin to explain we have about 37 pillows on the bed too, only two or three of which we use. As for me, I get by with my scruffy pillow I have used since childhood. (That's a slight exaggeration.)

Not long ago I was tidying up my corner of the den in preparation for the maid's visit the next day and thought of a spiritual parallel to my situation. God, through His grace, does the hard work of salvation by cleansing our souls from the stain sin. But when Christ comes into our hearts, we should want to do our part to make sure our lives are as "clean" as possible in anticipation of his return. Fortunately, I know when the maid is coming and I can clean up beforehand so the house is ready for her. The same can't be said for Jesus' return so it is incumbent on us to be clean and pure and expecting his return anytime.

Matthew 24:42 "Therefore keep watch, because you do not know on what day your Lord will come...44 So you also must be ready, because the Son of Man will come at an hour when you do not expect him."

Romance in the hospital waiting room

"For better or worse."

It was odd that I recalled my wedding vows during a recent trip to the hospital. Nancy and I have been married for 43 years and dating for almost a half a century. We had some romantic interludes in some exotic parts of the world in the past but recently, as new senior citizens, it seems our dates consist largely of accompanying each other to the hospital for some sort of test or the other. What these dates lack in romance they make up for in extravagant expenses.

"In sickness and in health."

Earlier this month we found ourselves at a local hospital after my doctor recommended a myelogram to take a closer look at what was causing the pain and numbness in my hands, arms and neck. A myelogram is an "invasive" procedure. If you're not up on your medical lingo that means your spinal column is "invaded" with an oversized needle, a foreign substance (some dye) is injected in an area of your body reserved for other fluids and some X-rays are taken.

Understandably this procedure required that I check into the hospital. Of course, being admitted into the hospital involves enough paperwork to make you sick if you weren't before you entered the hospital. The pleasant but officious young lady behind the counter began entering my information into the computer in a monotone voice reminiscent of a last conversation with a robot I saw watching Robocop.

"Last name?" "First Name?" "Middle Initial?" "Living Will?" "Say what??!!" "Living Will! Am I going to need a one?" I looked anxiously toward the door to see if I could make a getaway. Maybe my symptoms weren't so bad after all. Spending the rest of my life with numb arms didn't sound as bad as having my living will executed.

As the questioning continued, my stomach started growling. I hadn't been allowed to eat before the procedure. That was OK when the appointment was at 7:30 in the morning. Unfortunately, when it was moved to 11:30 that meant I was going to get really hungry. Ever the opportunist, I wondered if I could take credit for 12 hours of fasting that was a natural combination with the prayer I had been doing.

I know my doctor was just complying with the law and common sense when he reviewed all the dire warnings of things that might go wrong during surgery, but he practically scared me to death before he picked up the scalpel to begin the procedure. He said rather coolly, that I had a one in 50,000 chance of dying, a .06 percent chance of becoming a paraplegic and pretty good odds I'd die of sticker shock when I saw the bill.

The paperwork completed, I had next to select my outfit for the procedure. I was hoping for something in a herringbone or tweed. What I got was a pair of pants and hospital smock that I think was last worn by the "Biggest Loser" before he lost 350 pounds.

I entered the x-ray room a little dopey from the sedatives I had taken. The light was subdued and my doctor bore an eerie resemblance to Boris Karloff from a distance. He had me lie face down on a cold, hard table that looked a lot like a device I had seen in the dungeon of a medieval castle in England. I'm pretty sure the Geneva Convention bans such procedures in combat, but as long as you have a valid Medicare card, you're fair game in peacetime.

My head was contorted in the most uncomfortable positions imaginable, and I was advised to remain absolutely still. Then my doctor told me to relax. Relax?! You've gotta be kidding me! He said I was going to experience some "discomfort." That's doctor-speak for "this is going to hurt like Hades." I must confess that I had a difficult time relaxing while lying face down on a medieval implement of torture while Boris Karloff was poised over me with an oversized needle aimed at my spinal cord. He likened the pain I was about to experience to a bee sting. I had a flash back to the movie, "Return of the Killer Bees" and I braced myself for the shot. In truth, it wasn't that bad. I'm just a sissy.

Afterwards I was given an exciting gurney ride through the narrow halls of radiology returning to the recovery room where my bride was waiting. My nurse came in periodically to take my vitals. During this time Nancy and I enjoyed the intimacy of the moment, holding hands, staring blanking into my drug clouded eyes, the aroma of isopropyl alcohol in the air, amid shrill "Code Blue" PA announcements and medical people scurrying around officiously.

"Does it get any better than this?" I wondered out loud.

Finally, my nurse gave me my discharge instructions. I was to lie on my back for 48 hours of recovery. Nancy stated the obvious, "That will be hard for Don."

Our nurse understood and suggested that I just try not to think about work and maybe I could follow through on the doctor's instructions. "Good idea," I thought to myself, and went to the restroom having been confined to the gurney for a considerable time. In the restroom, I lifted the toilet seat and there in large print was the word "Church," as in Church Toilet Seat Company. Suddenly, I was involuntarily thinking about work again. This was going to be a long 48 hours.

In retrospect, it wasn't all that bad. I got a free meal, met some swell people and had a "date" with my girl.

"Till death do we part."

The recent health care debate highlighted how much we cherish good health. However, regardless of how superb our doctors and hospitals are, our bodies will eventually let us down and we will experience pain and discomfort. In fact, good health care merely postpones the inevitable. As believers we can look forward to a time when we won't have to put up with these annoying physical limitations.

Sometime in the future we will be issued a new body and won't have to experience these painful moments. At that time, "He will wipe every tear from their eyes. There will be no more death or mourning or crying or pain, for the old order of things has passed away." He who was seated on the throne said, "I am making everything new!" Revelation 21:4, 5

"What's in a name? A duck by any other name..."

I was fascinated by a recent *Outlook* article about a Kenyan woman who, when she was baptized, adopted the Christian name of Florence to signify her new life in Christ. I thought this was appropriate, and it got me to thinking about the role of names in our culture and my own experience with names.

"What's in a name?" mused Shakespeare, "That which we call a rose, by any other name would smell as sweet."

Perhaps the Bard could dismiss the importance of names in the 17th Century, but in the 21st names are the source of great confusion and concern. Last fall I watched a football game between the Indianapolis Colts and the Baltimore Ravens. Excuse me? Not that long ago it was the Baltimore Colts.

I can only imagine the enormous pressure on the committee designated to select the name of the new Baltimore football team. It had to select a name that wouldn't offend anyone. But what would former Baltimore resident Edgar Allen Poe say about the Ravens?..."nevermore," I suspect.

Baltimore's basketball team used to be the Bullets until they moved a few miles south and became the Washington

Bullets. If you ask me, the Washington Bullets never had the catchy ring of Baltimore Bullets, but it stuck until the late team owner Abe Pollen decided to change his team's name after 32 years.

I kid you not, someone thought that the team name sounded too violent. Abe was convinced that if they selected a kinder, gentler name like, maybe, The Washington Spitwads, that crime in the city would immediately plummet.

Aren't we carrying this PC thing a little far? Next thing you know burglars will demand that Pittsburgh change the name of its NFL team (think about it) and isn't the Minnesota NFL team a little unfair to Vikings? I've always objected to the New York Giants' name. It demeans the vertically challenged. Who speaks for us dwarfs?

My family has had a problem with names. Basically, we don't have much imagination. First there was Donald Ellis Waddell, Sr., my grandfather. Then, my dad Donald, Jr., was followed by yours truly, Don the III. Not to be outDonned (sic), Nancy and I named our first son Don the 4th. If you're following the pattern here, you may have already figured out that my grandson's name is Donald Ellis Waddell the Fifth.

For my part I've struggled less with my given name than I have with my nickname which, for as long as I can remember, has been "Duck." It was never my idea, Duck just stuck, so to speak. But, if your first name is "Donald" and your last name is most frequently mispronounced "waddle," you're probably going to be stuck with Duck whether you like it or not.

What's in a name? If you're talking about nicknames and sports teams, the answer is not much. If we're speaking about our Heavenly Father or His Son, names are very important and need to be used with respect. God's name was so sacred to the Jews that in Old Testament times they would not pronounce it out loud. The tetragrammation for God was YHWH, which would be written but not spoken.

(Vanna White hadn't arrived on scene yet to sell the Jews a vowel.) Interestingly, most scholars believe the vowels from Adonai were added to YHWH to give us the name of God, Jehovah. In most versions of the Bible, the word LORD (all caps) is used where YHWH or Jehovah was intended by the early Jews.

You can contrast this practice of treating God's name as sacred with today's flippant and often profane use. Tune in on a standard sitcom or listen to a game show where participants repeatedly say "Oh my God" and God lovers will be offended. It cheapens the sacredness of God, creator of the universe, when we use it unnecessarily and apart from reverence and worship. As much as I have heard God's name used in vain on TV and radio or listened to others say it profanely in the secular world, it still offends me because I know it cheapens the name of my LORD and Savior.

When you read the Bible you discover how very important one name in particular is: Jesus. As Paul wrote in Philippians 2:9: "Therefore God exalted him to the highest place and gave him a name that is above every name, that at the name of Jesus every knee should bow, in Heaven and on earth, and every tongue confess that Jesus Christ is Lord, to the glory of God the Father."

Names and name changes in the Bible other than Jesus are also important. Abram was renamed Abraham to mark the importance of his new role as a Patriarch and the covenantal relationship established between him and God. Likewise Jacob became known as Israel, the name of the land promised to the Jews by the Abrahamic covenant. Saul became Paul after his "Road to Damascus" experience.

A most significant Biblical name change was when Jesus designated that Simon would be known as "Cephas" meaning "Rock." The irony here is that during Jesus' life on this earth, Peter was anything but a "rock;" he was mercurial, impulsive, and often undependable under pressure. But

Jesus saw the potential in Peter who became rock solid in the book of Acts and helped the new movement of people named "Christians" explode into a revolution that changed people in the first Century and continues to change people today.

My prodigal daughter Dawn spent some time in a far off distant land slopping hogs until she found Christ at a hippie commune in California. When she returned home she was insistent that we call her by her first and middle name, "Dawn Michelle." I resisted for a while unwilling to change 30+ years of calling her Dawn until she explained that "Dawn" represented the old Dawn; "Dawn Michelle" was what she wanted to be called as a new creation in Jesus Christ. Cool! I get and respect that!!

What's in a name? According to the Bard, not much if we're talking about roses; if we're talking about people who take the name of Jesus, however, it makes an eternal difference.

A regular spiritual exercise program will help you live longer, a lot longer

*For physical training is of some value, but godliness
has value for all things, holding promise for both
the present life and the life to come.---1 Timothy 4:8*

I have been a runner most of my life. When you're my size it's a good thing to be a step faster than any potential predator or adversary. In high school I was a sprinter until I lit up a Marlboro at the track banquet to the dismay of our coach Mr. Ash. Concluding that it was probably too late, he didn't admonish me that cigarettes would stunt my growth.

But in 1972, after ten years of coughing and hacking, I finally quit smoking during my year in Vietnam and began running regularly, mostly to stay in shape. My hobby turned into a passion and soon I was running 10k's, half-marathons and ultimately three full marathons. My favorite was the Marine Corps marathon in Washington, DC, the last half-mile of which was uphill...only the Marines would do that. The most memorable race was the half-marathon through

Berlin, just after the wall came down and the city was reunified.

I also competed in several Derby Festival mini-Marathons. Midway in my training program in 1997 my sedentary wife, Nancy, ever the encourager, asked: "Why are you going to wake up before sunrise, travel across town, wedge yourself amongst thousands of other scantily clad people, huddling nervously in what is usually a chilly April morning and completely exhaust yourself by running 13.1 miles? That's stupid." I couldn't think of a really good answer off the top of my head. But after considering the question, I finally came up with three reasons I have been a runner most of my life.

I share this with you because I am a great proponent of regular exercise and believe everyone can benefit from a sensible, regular exercise program. (See a doctor first if you're just getting started!). But there is also a wonderful spiritual application to be made that can help us grow as Christians. I run because:

1. It helps me control my weight. When I started running 39 years ago, I weighed in at a hefty 175 pounds (20 more than I currently weigh), but since then I have maintained weight in the 150s. We all know that any form of exercise burns calories. Running consumes about 100 calories per mile so every 36 miles burns about a pound of fat. Another way to look at it is that I can eat two more donuts every day I run. That tends to add up over time especially since I came to work at Southeast where donuts seem to be a staple of our diet.

I did some rough calculations and determined that if I had not run about 15 miles a week for the past four decades and had not altered my eating habits during that period I would now weigh about 520 pounds more than I presently weigh. I suspect an additional quarter of a ton on my 5'5" frame might make me look a tad on the hefty side.

2. It makes me feel better afterwards. Not only does exercise elevate your energy level, but after about 20 minutes of running, your body starts to produce endorphins, a morphine derivative. This promotes what's called the "runner's high." If you don't exactly feel euphoric afterwards, it at least reduces the pain! I know how Bob Russell feels about running. He says that since he never sees anybody smiling while they run, he concludes it can't be that much fun. Actually we runners don't smile because we don't want to get bugs in our teeth. If Bob only knew we are mainlining endorphins, he might join us for a jog. Nah.

I'm sure you heard of the preacher who wasn't feeling well. He went to the doctor who prescribed exercise. The doctor told the minister: "Run five miles a day and call me back in two weeks." The minister did exactly as he was instructed. He called the doctor back two weeks later and said: "OK, Doc, I'm 70 miles from home, what should I do now?"

3. Studies suggest that regular exercise may lead to a longer life. The evidence isn't conclusive but it is compelling. People who are active and exercise regularly tend to live longer than sedentary people. Nancy cynically reminds me that that means I'll probably spend those additional years cooped up in a nursing home with some church volunteer wiping slobber off my chin.

In writing to Timothy, Paul acknowledged the value of a regular exercise program. But he also knew that our physical bodies are less important than our spiritual bodies and that our spiritual bodies need exercise too. If we don't exercise our physical bodies, they will gradually deteriorate and perhaps die prematurely. The same is true of your spiritual body that needs to stay in shape through prayer, worship and regular Bible study. If you keep up an active spiritual workout program you will feel better and most assuredly live longer--- a lot longer...like forever.

Men, surprise your wife. Do something thoughtful for Valentine's Day

This year, I thought I'd do something new and unexpected for Valentine's Day. I did something thoughtful. This is so not me. Usually I pick up a card or some candy at Walgreens on the way home from work. Flowers are nice, I am told, but oh so expensive and every time I bring home a new computer, golf club or some technical gadget or do dad, Nancy chides me about the need to save money. So in the past I've cut back on Valentine's Day.

I'm not an overly romantic type guy normally. I think I'm generous and always want to be helpful, but when it comes to making a big deal about some Hallmark-invented holiday, I generally have something better to do. Now Nancy tells me that she feels loved, respected and valued, and I am inclined to believe her since we've been married for 44 years and she hasn't killed me yet. I know it's crossed her mind, however.

For our 25th wedding anniversary, I took Nancy to romantic Bavaria and a wonderful Alpine resort nestled at the foot of the Austrian Alps. What more could a girl want?

Did I mention that it was a five day golf outing... and Nancy doesn't golf. I tried to make it up to her with a wonderful evening in Innsbruck---4 star restaurant, evening stroll under the stars, that sort of thing.

Later when we returned to our hotel room I found her staring wistfully off into the starlit sky, and I put my hand on her shoulder knowing she was reflecting on 25 years of marital bliss with someone as special as I and asked, "What are you thinking about, honey?" "It just occurred to me," she purred "if I had killed you the first time I thought about it, I'd be out of jail by now."

Nancy graciously allowed me a do-over for our 25th anniversary.

But in terms of an extravagant display of love, nothing rivaled Valentine's Day 2010. We were planning a getaway for a couple of days at a Bed and Breakfast as we do regularly, but we couldn't find one that would take dogs and our normal dog sitter wasn't available. Then I had this brilliant plan, which I managed to keep secret.

We had already planned to go out to an elegant restaurant for dinner. While Nancy was preoccupied with her weekly, sacrosanct Friday trip to the beauty parlor, I decorated the upstairs guest room in appropriate Valentine's Day décor. I took out a second mortgage on our house and purchased a dozen red roses and strategically placed strawberry scented candles around the room. A large Valentine's Day balloon moored to the flowers bobbed gracefully in the air.

I had a bottle of bubbly on ice (non-alcoholic in case any elders are reading) and spread dozens of brightly colored Valentine candies on the bed. No sooner had I turned my back than I perceived a white streak making a supersonic beeline to the bed. I spun around to find Zac, our nine-year-old Bichon diving in the middle of the candy-laden bed and helping himself to the chocolates. "Zac!" I shouted, "you just had your teeth cleaned yesterday (true story), your den-

85

tist would not approve." Too quick for this 64 year old, Zac darted down the stairs with several aluminum foil wrapped chocolates in his mouth. (I have since learned that large amounts of chocolate can make a dog very sick.)

That night after we returned home from eating out, I announced to Nancy that I had found a "Bed and Breakfast" that takes dogs. She looked puzzled as I walked her up the stairs to our guestroom-turned romantic B&B.

I had prepared a slide show of pictures of Nancy and me over the past 46 years to the tune of Kenny Rogers, "Through the Years." Then, the *piece de resistance*: I had found a VCR copy of the movie "A Man and a Woman," the movie we watched in 1967 just before we were engaged. We watched it again and Nancy melted in my arms like a piece of Valentine's Day candy in Zac's mouth.

Stunned and surprised seem inadequate to describe her reaction to my romantic initiative. Nancy was quite literally speechless. When I saw the tears, I knew I had hit a home run. I took this as a positive reaction until it occurred to me that it is not necessarily a good thing when doing something thoughtful surprises your spouse.

The Bible sets a high standard for husbands in loving their wives. Ephesians 5:25, 26: "Husbands, love your wives, just as Christ loved the church and gave himself up for her... husbands ought to love their wives as their own bodies." I have fallen short of this lofty goal, and while I have probably done an adequate job in providing for Nancy in tangible terms, I need to a better job of showing my love in impractical, romantic ways that will serve to strengthen our relationship.

Any landing you can walk away from is a good one... and other myths

"Gear down and locked." I announced to Chuck my navigator, a.k.a. GIB (guy in back), or WSO (weapons systems operator.)

"Roger, three green," he responded confirming three green lights on his gear indicator panel. It was April 4, 1972 and Chuck was about to complete his final combat mission before returning home to America. He was winding up a year in war-ravaged Vietnam while I still had eight months to go. It would be a monumental understatement to say I was homesick. I missed my family so much it hurt, even while I found flying combat exhilarating.

We had just completed a "routine" night combat mission, if any combat or night mission can be called routine. I was still excited about the great missions we completed the day before, one of which would result in my being awarded a Distinguished Flying Cross. Since the weather was solid from the ground to 12,000 feet we opted for a "combat sky spot" weapons delivery.

A ground radar site located somewhere in South Vietnam guided our two-ship flight of F-4 Phantoms to a point in the sky and ordered us to release our bombs over a suspected enemy target. The controller ordered crisply, "30 seconds to bomb release...standby to release on my mark...ready, ready, pickle." (The term "pickle" means for a fighter pilot to release his bombs and originated on practice bombing ranges before World War Two when bombs hitting their target were described as dropping into a pickle barrel.)

Twenty-four 500-pound bombs began their brief flight to the earth. According to the intelligence briefing, we received before flight, the target was listed as an enemy concentration but in all likelihood the enemy had long since found a safer haven. It was more probable that our ordnance simply converted a couple of dozen trees into toothpicks and left a community of monkeys with their ears ringing. Regardless, Chuck reminded me to safe my weapons panel and vector home to DaNang where we would begin the most hazardous portion of our flight, landing at night on DaNang's notoriously slippery runway.

The pace of flight operations during the Vietnam War had not allowed maintenance crews to remove tire rubber that had accumulated on the runway thus making the surface treacherous. That evening the preflight weather briefing hadn't been too encouraging with the possibility of thunderstorms in the forecast. Standard operations under these circumstances was to engage the barrier or cable that lay across the runway with the aircraft tailhook to bring the aircraft to a safe stop.

As we made our approach to land, a thunderstorm had indeed parked itself over the runway reducing visibility and leaving puddles of water on the tarmac. A further distraction was the potential for antiaircraft fire that was occasionally aimed at U.S. aircraft landing at DaNang. Diverting to an alternate field in Thailand was a possibility, but foul weather and low fuel made that option iffy at best. We were about one mile from touchdown when I picked up the runway strobe lights by squinting out the rain-obscured side panel of the canopy. Lined up slightly right at 150 knots, I made one slight correction and touched down, hard but safe. I lowered the tail hook, which would engage the barrier and bring the aircraft to a sudden but safe stop and thus conclude Chuck's final flight and my 60th combat mission.

Unfortunately, I had not perceived a slight right to left drift at touchdown and the aircraft departed the runway just six feet before the cable. Landing gear designed for use on prepared surfaces do not operate well on grass and the resulting ride was brief but terrifying. All three landing gear were torn away from the undercarriage and the $3 million aircraft came to rest with a portion of its undercarriage stuck in the mud. Instincts took over as I performed an emergency ground egress and dashed away from the Phantom whose right engine was still running. Safely away from the machine, I observed Chuck still in the cockpit struggling with his harness so I returned to assist him and while I was in the vicinity shut down the engine that was still running.

To this day I can vividly remember the sickening feeling deep within my gut as I stood in the pouring rain and watched emergency vehicles tend to the wreckage. I had destroyed a perfectly good multimillion-dollar jet and almost killed my backseater and myself. I can never recall feeling a deeper sense of despair. Surely my career as a pilot was over. Perhaps I'd have to leave the Air Force. What then? It is an understatement to say that my self-confidence had taken a severe, perhaps mortal blow. I did what most do in similar circumstances. I prayed. It was a pitiful prayer actually but it was most sincere, and from my perspective a quarter of a century later I can say that it was answered.

The rain continued at a steady pace as I watched emergency crews secure the aircraft accident site, my aircraft accident. The unit's safety team had been awakened in the middle of the night to begin the tedious and painstaking task of piecing together what really happened so that they might assign blame where appropriate and determine what mistakes had been made in the hope that such errors would not be repeated by some future aviator.

I could have saved them the trouble because I knew what mistakes had been made. Basically, I screwed up. While trying to land in marginal weather conditions after a night combat mission I had not perceived a slight right to left skid and the aircraft departed the runway prior to taking the barrier. End of story.

I tried to comfort myself by reviewing all the mitigating factors---I was a new pilot with only a couple of hundred hours in this plane, the weather was bad, the runway slippery...none of my rationalizing changed the facts. I had destroyed a perfectly good jet, a $3,000,000 F-4D Phantom to be precise, and now I had to consider how this event would affect the rest of my life.

There is an adage in the flying business that "Any landing you can walk away from is a good landing." Since this saying was popularized when aircraft cost thousands rather than millions of dollars, try as I might I couldn't find anyone who subscribed to this particular line of reasoning. After the accident I attained instant celebrity status. Even the wing commander, who never had spoken to me before, now knew my name.

For a while I was the topic of conversation at the bar and my reputation as an aviator, so important to a fighter pilot, took a hit. I was certainly no longer Sierra Hotel*. I was pretty sure I had joined the ranks of Whiskey Delta.* (* That's fighter pilot speak that when cleaned up for polite company means "Exceptional Aviator" and "Weak Jock" or words to that effect.)

It is customary for pilots involved in an accident to be grounded until the accident investigation is completed. However, my commander, General George Rutter took a chance and let me fly two days later. Since the mission's target that day was located deep in the heart of Hanoi, at the time the most heavily defended area in the world, I wondered if he was trying to rebuild my confidence or just trying to get rid of me. Actually, it was a great confidence builder, and I deeply appreciate the risk he took. Others tried to console me in various ways. The maintenance officer was ebullient at the thought of stripping the now "unairworthy" aircraft. "Just think of all the spare parts you gave us." I was disconsolate, but thanked him anyway.

What lessons did I learn from this ordeal? I think Luke 18:1 sums it up nicely. "Then Jesus told his disciples a parable to show them that they should always pray and not give up."

Lesson 1. Always pray. As I stood in rain and observed the sleek, graceful fighter now stuck in the mud, I uttered a pitiful but sincere prayer. "God help me." I didn't realize it then, but I do realize now that He did help me. Not only does the act of praying help in soliciting God's assistance in times of trial, but it also keeps our focus in the right person, God.

That's why Paul writes that we should "give thanks in all circumstances" and "pray without ceasing." If we always fix our eyes on Jesus and pray, we'll understand that regardless of the circumstances, it will all work out in the end, because "we know that in all things God works for the good of those who love him, who have been called according to his purpose." Romans 8: 28

Lesson 2. Never give up. I was tempted to throw in the towel many times over the course of the next couple of years but somehow I persevered with the Lord's help. On April 4, 1972 I considered getting out of the Air Force because of my accident, but on November 8th of that year, I completed my combat tour with 151 missions, two Distinguished Flying Cross and nine Air Medals.

Two years later I got some "lucky breaks" and was selected to the prestigious job of instructor pilot in my new unit. In 1980, the Chief of Staff of the Air Force presented me the award as the "Best F-15 Pilot In Europe." In August of 1995, I completed a very successful, 28-year Air Force career culminating as a command pilot, colonel and wing commander. Though it wasn't easy overcoming the past, I'm glad now I persisted, that I didn't give up.

Lesson 3. Trust God, just trust God. Surely this is the lesson Job learned, and it is the lesson I am still learning. When things are going well and you're flying high, trust God. When you're surveying the wreckage of a fighter jet you just destroyed, a relationship you messed up or some personal endeavor gone wrong, trust God, just trust God. That is the only hope in our life. Paul described my situation precisely when he wrote in Romans "Not only so, but we also rejoice in our sufferings, because we know that suffering produces perseverance; perseverance, character; and character, hope. And hope does not disappoint us, because God has poured out his love into our hearts by the Holy Spirit, whom he has given us." Romans 5:3-5

As I look back from my current situation over 40 years later, I wouldn't change a thing since I have been so blessed in my life and ministry. Maybe it was a good landing after all.

To the Thessalonians Paul wrote: "Be joyful always; pray continually; give thanks in all circumstances, for this is God's will for you in Christ Jesus." 1 Thessalonians 5:16-18

May he rest in peace, right after his ex beats up his other ex

I always thought it curious that ministers speak of "officiating" at a funeral. I mean it makes it sound like an NCAA basketball game or a WWF wrestling match. Some years ago, however, I "officiated" at a funeral that helped me better understand why that term might be more appropriate than I thought.

I arrived early and talked to the funeral home owner who told me that he regularly had to call the cops to intervene in fights between grieving family members. (I sometimes exaggerate in my column but this is the Gospel truth…so to speak.) The week before this particular funeral, the funeral home director had to call the police because a fight broke out in the women's restroom between the deceased's two ex-wives.

These "ladies" were slugging it out in the restroom, their natural animosity exaggerated by the fact that they had just discovered that the deceased had left everything he owned (pickup truck, some money, two lottery tickets and a "Go Big Blue" sweat shirt) to his new girlfriend and not to either of them.

Armed with this new information, I began the eulogy. In retrospect the funeral would have gone a lot better, had I gotten the name of the deceased correct. As I waded into the eulogy, one of the family members, a rather large, young, male adult who had previously been talking on his cellphone during the reading of the 23rd Psalm, got out of his seat and approached me in a menacing manner.

I eyed the fire exit in case I had to make a hurried exit least I be drug into the ladies restroom for a beating. "Can I help you?" I said, my voice trembling. "I just wanted you to know that his name was Rob not Bob." Now in fact, I had misspoken, but corrected myself immediately. Apparently the family member missed my correction, while talking on his cellphone.

In any event, the remainder of the funeral went well and I think we honored the deceased, comforted he bereaved and praised the Lord without any fisticuffs in the ladies restroom.

For the record I do not like doing funerals even when the police aren't involved. Generally I have little time to prepare for the event and more often than not it is not a happy occasion. At the same time, I have learned that funerals are a great opportunity to minister to those in need and to share the Gospel. After a decade of doing funerals, I have determined there are at least three reasons that I can't say "no" when someone asks me to conduct a funeral.

1. It is an honor to preside over this ceremony, one of life's most significant events. Often when I minister to someone in need I'm unsure if I really helped. That is not the case with a funeral. People are grieving, they are hurting and we get to ease the pain by being there for them, listening, and comforting them with the soothing words of Scripture that assist them through the grieving process.

2 Corinthians 1:3,4, "Praise be to the God and Father of our Lord Jesus Christ, the Father of compassion and the God of all comfort, who comforts us in all our troubles, so that

we can comfort those in any trouble with the comfort we ourselves have received from God."

2. I always enjoy honoring the deceased by recounting major events in his or her life. To that end, I interview as many family members as I can and try to get to know the deceased. Invariably, I wished I had gotten to know the person better while they were alive. There is a lesson here for all of us: We need to venerate our relationships and seek to know friends and family members better while they (and we) are alive.

3. Finally, funerals are a great time to share the Gospel when the participants in the service are particularly receptive to its message of hope beyond the grave and the reminder of the brevity of life. Barring the second return Christ, we all will wind up where the deceased is. We will die and be put into a coffin. Friends will gather to pay their last respects. A minister will speak inspiring words of comfort. Faced with this inevitability, a funeral reminds us that life is short. A funeral reminds us that we are lost without a savior.

But there is hope for all those who place their trust in Christ. John 14:1 "Do not let your hearts be troubled. Trust in God; trust also in me. 2 In my Father's house are many rooms; if it were not so, I would have told you. I am going there to prepare a place for you. 3 And if I go and prepare a place for you, I will come back and take you to be with me that you also may be where I am."

Fortunately, all my recent funerals have been dignified affairs uninterrupted by 911 calls or the police. I've also managed to get the name of the deceased correct most of the time.

Husband lost on aisle nine

In the summer of 2011, my wife Nancy experienced one of her infrequent MS exacerbations and was essentially bedridden for five months.

As if battling multiple sclerosis for the past 47 years wasn't bad enough, Nancy has also recently been diagnosed with kidney disease, anemia and high blood pressure. Not too surprisingly, Nancy's health challenges have put quite a dent in our social life. Our idea of a date has morphed into a trip to the doctor's and holding hands in the waiting room. I am never sure whether her dreamy-eyed looks were romantic glances or just the cloudy glaze brought on by her medication.

Naturally, with Nancy laid up in bed I have to take up the slack, washing the dishes, cleaning, or doing the laundry. I have renewed appreciation for my bride's hard work over the years and I'm grateful for our daughter Dawn Michelle pitching in. Best of all, I think I'm back in contention to become the Holly Point Condo Association Husband of the Year for 2011.

Aside from doing housework, I also go to the grocery, which is one of my least favorite activities in the whole world. Cleaning the septic tank with a toothbrush or listening to old State of the Union speeches isn't even a close second to my distaste for shopping.

However, as a former Boy Scout and career Air Force officer, I will do my duty; I just want to be allowed to whine about it in my *Outlook* column. So off I trundled to my neighborhood Kroger with Nancy's hand-scrawled shopping list. To her credit she had categorized the list into food groups, which would have been more helpful had not our local grocery reorganized their store layout since my last visit.

My first stop was fruit and vegetables where I encountered a problem. Do I buy organic or... what's the alternative, inorganic? Isn't an inorganic vegetable a contradiction in terms? Using my iPhone, I went to the internet to find out more information. One site explained the top ten reasons to buy organic, but they did not mention that organic is substantially more expensive. A *Business Week* article maintained that organic was good for children and pregnant women, and since I did not qualify in either category, I hustled to the cheaper non-organic, cariogenic, "normal" fruit and vegetables.

Next on my list, Nancy had written, "Bread - mine and yours." Say what? His and her bread? I understand about his and her towels, TV remotes, and coffee cups but "his and her bread?" She likes 100 percent whole wheat; I like white bread refined, bleached with extra endosperm. Nancy's bread tastes a little like a cross between sawdust and cardboard and leaves pieces of stuff stuck in my teeth. I thought I was really clever when I filled a Ziplock baggie with sawdust and wrote "Nancy's bread" on the outside. I attributed her adverse response to my joke to a side effect of one of her medications.

My mind was still reeling from the complexity of contending with organic vegetables, when I found myself in the clothes washing detergent aisle. I was bewildered by the number of choices, and struggled to decipher Nancy's handwriting. It said "Tide" something. That wasn't much help. There was Tide Original Scent, Tide Free, Mountain Spring, Tide plus Febreze, Tide Free and Gentle. Whatever happened to just plain "Tide"?

Finally I closed my eyes and grabbed a bottle at random figuring, actually quite wrongly I later learned, Nancy wouldn't notice. This mistake earned me a return trip to Kroger, and I missed a full quarter of the Slippery Rock and Armadillo College football game. I got Tide Free and Gentle, even if the scolding I got from my bride was free but not so gentle.

Actually laundry detergent was easy next to buying cereal. I counted 182 cereal options. You've got to be kidding me. Remember when life was simpler, when our breakfast choices were basically Sugar Pops, Rice Krispies, and Cheerios. My 88-year old mother put it in perspective. She could remember all the way back to BC...Before Cheerios! I think she said her choices as a young lady were porridge, gruel or grits.

Overall, our shopping choices are incredibly plentiful. I think of it as consumerism run amok, and it's easy to focus only on the choices and forget the godly virtues of self-restraint and discipline. With all the choices we get to make as consumers is there any wonder we have so many overweight, self-indulgent people?

That's bad enough, but there is a danger when we allow a consumer mindset to invade our church. We begin to think the church is here to satisfy our needs, to offer us a variety of options we want. We want the programming we desire. We become critical when the music isn't to our liking. I've heard of some members who don't attend church when their preferred preacher isn't speaking.

This is not the way it should be. Christ hasn't called us to be Christian consumers, to go to church to have our needs met and choose from a vast array of spiritual choices and church programs. Unlike the grocery or the mall, the church is a place we go to meet Jesus and then focus on meeting the needs of others, not having our needs met. Jesus said:

"If any man will come after me, let him deny himself, and take up his cross daily, and follow me." Luke 9:23

If there's such a thing as "Hurry Sickness," I am terminally ill

S ome time ago, I read John Ortberg's book, *The Life You've Always Wanted*, where he talks about the "Hurry Sickness." It is an area I struggle with in my own life since I stay pretty busy, and I think my hyper busyness may interfere with my relationship with God. As I conducted my research, I discovered that many others suffer from the same malady; so much so that some experts are maintaining that as a culture we are experiencing a "Hurry Sickness Epidemic."

In the following I will make three main points. Even though I've never been to Bible College I know that there is an immutable theological principle that all good written or spoken items in the church have three main points. The best sermons have three main points that begin with the same letter, but that refinement is beyond my ecclesiastical abilities.

The symptoms of the Hurry Sickness are easy to recognize. In its more innocent forms, we observe people who get impatient waiting for emails to download, get frustrated by traffic jams or regularly talk on the cellphone while driving and eating a Big Mac (I've never done this, but I know some people who have!). People get hurt in the more serious manifestations of the disease such as road rage, airplane rage or supermarket rage. I once read a Breakpoint article, "Express Line Rage," which told of a Boston lady who beat another woman senseless in a supermarket parking lot because the lady had one more item in her shopping basket than was allowed in the express lane.

How do you diagnosis this disease? It almost goes without saying that if you find yourself counting the items in the basket of the person in front of you in the grocery express line, and it leads to fisticuffs in the parking lot, you're probably sick.

1) Ortberg asks, when you come to a red light on a four-lane road with a car in each lane, do you try to figure out which car will pull away faster, and try to get in that lane? If you are fortunate to get behind Dave Stone you're sure to get away quickly and maybe get a speeding ticket as well. 2) Do you try to figure out which line in the supermarket is going to move faster, and then while in line monitor the other line to see how you would have done so you can choose better next time? 3) Do you multitask by driving, eating, talking on the cellphone and putting on make-up? 4) Do you live or work surrounded by clutter? (Perhaps John has seen my desk at work.) 5) Do you come home exhausted and unable to give your best to the people you are supposed to care for the most?

After reading Ortberg's book, I decided I had a terminal case of the hurry sickness. So what's the cure? There are four remedies, I think. One, we should follow the Biblical admonition to remember the Sabbath and keep it holy. Since we live under the new Covenant, we are less constrained to a particular day than we are to have a weekly time of rest and recovery.

Two, as God wrote through the Psalmist: "Be still and know that I am God." This is where I struggle most, since it's so incredibly difficult for me to be still and not be dashing around with my hair on fire (figuratively speaking of course since I'm bald) trying to do more stuff than is sensible. I first recognized this about myself when I read the quote about me in my 1963 high school annual, which said "I'd rather be sick than idle."

Three, we need to be more like Mary and less like Martha. In the tenth chapter of his Gospel Luke tells about Christ visiting the home of Mary and Martha. Martha is afflicted with the hurry sickness. While Mary is sitting at Jesus' feet, Martha complains that she should be helping her work in the kitchen. Jesus tells Martha to "chill out," (that's from the WPV or the "Waddell Paraphrase Version" of the Bible). I need to be more like Mary, spending time with the Master, and less like Martha who was busy doing less important stuff.

Four, we need to follow Christ's example, who in his brief time on earth invested time in relationships, rested often, went to parties, and often sought solitude to be alone with his Father, such as Gethsemane and after feeding the 5000.

I spoke on a Wednesday night at church about the "hurry sickness," and I confessed that I don't spend as much time in solitude as I should. I pledged to spend more time alone with God and to report back what I discovered in my time of increased solitude. Here's what I did.

I set aside an hour a day to be alone with God. My daily quiet time usually runs from 20-30 minutes and includes Scripture reading and prayer. In the week following my sermon, I spent an hour in the sanctuary alone on one day, an hour praying at home the next, and I later spent an hour reading Psalms. One morning I listened to worship CDs for an hour in my office. The time passed quickly but I got horse from singing at the top of my lungs. Fortunately it was early and I didn't frighten anyone except security and a few custodial people.

Here's what I learned in my experiment with solitude.

1. The most important thing we can do is to make a daily appointment with God and keep it. The length of time is less important than the regularity. For me that time has to be in the morning before I get distracted by other activities and before I get so tired I can't concentrate. I now believe that longer times of solitude alone with God are important and I plan to do that periodically in the future. Not long ago I went on a "Desert Day" to our Christian Retreat Center where I spent an entire day fasting, praying, worshipping and reading God's word.

2. As Ortberg said in his book, we must ruthlessly eliminate hurry in our lives. Carl Jung, the Austrian psychologists said: "Hurry is not of the Devil; hurry is the Devil." During the week after my Wednesday evening talk, I consciously slowed down. I discovered this was more an attitude change than a change in practice. I found that I had more time for relationships and more time to be attuned to what God would have me do.

3. If we maintain balance in our life, there's nothing wrong with being busy, productive and purposeful. I like the Erik Liddell quote in *Chariots of Fire*: "When I run I feel God's pleasure." Often when I'm working hard on a project, I feel God's pleasure. The key is making sure it's God's work and not mine I'm doing. I can only tell the difference if I have spent time alone with God beforehand.

The day after I spoke at chapel, my dad stopped by my office at church and asked if I wanted to go out for lunch. I looked at my "to do" list and the mountain of paperwork in my in basket, and whereas I might have declined a month ago, I grabbed my coat and said: "Sure, let's go. You can buy." I also grabbed my cellphone just in case Dave Stone called me for advice on his next sermon series.

The theology of bumper stickers

Each election year cycle I see more and more bumper stickers asking that I vote for a particular candidate. After the election those who win proudly keep their bumper sticker on their car while the losers exchange theirs for one that says "Don't blame me I voted for _____." Fill in the blank with the loser of your choice.

I am a connoisseur of bumper stickers and get a kick out of many that I have read. I saw one not long ago that was a mild critique of my previous 28 years of service in the armed forces. It said: "War never solved anything." Soon afterwards I saw the alternative message that told the rest of the story: "Except for ending slavery, fascism, Nazism and Communism, war has never solved anything."

These concise, simplistic expressions got me thinking about other bumper stickers I've seen. Consider how helpful the following examples are: "Be nice to your kids. They'll choose you're nursing home." "The Lottery: A tax on people who are bad at math." "Give me ambiguity or give me something else." "Warning: dates on the calendar are closer than they appear." "Forget about world peace, visualize your turn signal." And the especially provocative: "Aren't you glad your mom was pro-life."

Just for fun I have compiled a list of my favorite bumper stickers, which I'll count down Dave Letterman style.

Bumper sticker Number 10. "My son is an honor student at _____ Elementary School." This sort of immodesty really galls me. My parents would never have displayed such a tacky, self-promoting sticker...probably because their oldest son never qualified as an honor student. I rather like the Nietzschesque sticker that says, "My son can beat up your honor student," or the one I saw recently, "My son is an honor student at the State Correctional Facility." Now there's a proud parent to be sure.

Number 9 comes from misguided animal rights activists. "Love animals, don't eat them." I rather agree with the antithetical bumper sticker: "If we aren't supposed to eat animals, why are they made of meat?" or "I didn't fight my way to the top of the food chain to be a vegetarian."

Number 8. "Don't laugh at least it's paid for." This one is usually affixed to a vehicle that looks like it rode out Hurricane Katrina and invariably has a "Go Big Blue" bumper sticker attached to the same bumper.

Number 7. "My other car is a Mercedes." Some time ago, I saw the "other" car, honest. It was a black Mercedes SL500 convertible driving down Shelbyville Road. The license plate read "NBA MOM." I thought to myself, "that says it all."

Number 6. "I'd rather be _____ (choose one), flying, sailing, sky diving, etc." The way many of these guys drive, I'd rather they were doing something else too.

Number 5. "Save energy, buy American." Nice thought, I guess; but I saw this one recently on Shelbyville Road affixed to a large, gas-guzzling, foreign made SUV. This reminded me of a car we bought while stationed in Germany. It was a 1990 Honda, a Japanese car, made in Ohio, and sold in Germany.

Bumper sticker number 4. These were very popular some years ago. "_____ (fill in the blank) do it better." I never had the courage to ask what "it" was, but since so many people were doing it so well, whatever "it" was, it couldn't be that special.

Number 3. "I (heart symbol) _____ (fill in the blank.)" The noun which goes in the blank of this facile statement is usually some obscure animal or vegetable no one in their right mind would brag about in polite company. Something like "I (heart symbol) Tasmanian pomegranates" or "I (heart symbol) Wirehaired Shetland Poodles," or some such.

Number 2. "Practice random acts of kindness and senseless acts of beauty." I first saw this on a car driven by a 20-something flower child who cut across three lanes of traffic to make an illegal turn on to the expressway. I thought to myself well that wasn't a random act of kindness so it must have been a senseless act of beauty. Personally, I don't recommend senseless acts of beauty when you're behind the wheel, but some acts of kindness would be appreciated.

And finally my all-time favorite bumper sticker. Drum roll, please.

Bumper sticker number 1: "In case of the rapture this vehicle will be unoccupied." I am a premillennialist myself, but I still think this sticker sounds a tad presumptuous. This is the spiritual equivalent to "Na-na-na-na-na-na."

In the final analysis, bumper stickers attempt to do three things, I think. 1. They proclaim our identity with a specific group or organization. 2. Bumper stickers tell the world how special we or the members of our family are. 3. They attempt to express a philosophy of life in ten words or less.

I never had a bumper sticker on my car until I returned to Louisville in 1995. My mom gave me a "Southeast Christian Church" bumper sticker, told me to put it on my car, and, valuing my inheritance, I complied.

A funny thing happened when I put that sticker on my car. I became more conscious of the fact that my driving reflected not only on me but my church, and I was compelled to drive in a more courteous manner. I was less likely to cut people off in traffic and I kept my speed down. I resisted the temptation to shake my fist at some of the buffoons who occupy our nation's highways.

In a very real sense, Christians have a figurative bumper sticker on our person that identifies us with our Lord. Others are judging us, our church and our Lord by what we say and the way we act. Paul put it this way in 2 Corinthians 4:10: "We always carry around in our body the death of Jesus, so that the life of Jesus may also be revealed in our body."

Makes me wonder what sort of Jesus am I revealing by the bumper sticker on my car or the life I am living each day?

Once a proud Colonel, I'm now just a Holy gofer

I was scurrying out of the Ministry Resource Center recently when I bumped into Nancy Aguiar, the perpetually bubbly, spirit-filled wife of our Chief of Security, Ron Aguiar. "Colonel, where are you going in such a hurry?" she asked.

"I'm going to pick up some make-up for Bob Russell," I replied. Nancy gave me a "you gotta be kidding me" look, so I stopped to explain. "He's taping his latest DVD in the Matthew series and his usual cosmetologist is out of town, so I've got to get the make up to him for tonight's taping."

I realize as a man, having a cosmetologist is not exactly, well, manly, but is necessary when in front of the camera. As Bob's Administrative Assistant (read "secretary" absent the skirt) it was my duty to pick up the makeup and get it to the "church/studio on time" for the shooting.

Nancy winked at me, and I knew what she was thinking. She often calls me "Colonel" recalling my days in the military where, as a "full bird" Colonel, I enjoyed a certain status that did not require running errands for a civilian. As a wing commander, I had 2500 people working for me, a budget of $220,000,000 and was responsible for one-third of the nuclear weapons in Europe. Now I am responsible for getting make-up for Bob Russell.

I was struck by the irony of the current situation and reflected upon my days as an officer in the Air Force. At that time I was obsessed with the concept of being "upwardly mobile," meaning I was on an upward vector to promotions, new career opportunities, higher pay and greater status. Matter of fact, when I went through Officer's Training School, we had a class where a senior officer talked about a career in the Air Force and assisted us in mapping out our career from 2nd Lieutenant to 4 star-general.

I wrote down years 1-30 horizontally across a sheet of paper and then entered certain prerequisites at the appropriate time. I'd graduate from pilot training, spend two tours as a pilot perfecting my expertise, attend Air Command and Staff College, serve a tour in the Pentagon, become a squadron commander, attend Air War College, then fly, then back to the Pentagon, eventually leading to my promotion to General Officer. I told myself I only desired promotion to enhance my Christian witness. Yeah, right!

Actually it didn't work out that way. Despite all the career planning, countless hours of conniving, maneuvering for the best jobs, and endearing myself to the right senior officers, I never got promoted to General. You see while I was praying to get promoted to General, my wife Nancy, who abhorred the thought of all the additional social duties associated with being the wife of a General, was praying that I not get promoted. Since she's always been more spiritual than I, she prevailed.

To be perfectly honest, I don't think I had the "right stuff" to be a General. To be even more transparent, I thank God almost daily that it worked out the way it did. You see I love serving as the New Member Minister at Southeast Christian Church, and I thank God it worked out the way it did.

While the world stresses career advancement and being upwardly mobile, the essence of the Christian life is just the opposite: It's about humility and the Bible is rife with examples of godly men who thought less about "career" advancement and more about how they could honor God by being obedient to God. Abraham left his hometown of Ur and followed God's lead to a far off land. John the Baptist's profile diminished when Jesus came on the scene and eclipsed John's popularity. Of course Jesus clearly demonstrated "downward mobility" when he left Heaven to live in the squalor and corruption of this fallen world.

In doing so He taught us about the humility required to be a follower of Jesus. Writing to the church at Philippi, Paul said: "Your attitude should be the same as that of Christ Jesus: Who, being in very nature God, did not consider equality with God something to be grasped, but made himself nothing, taking the very nature of a servant, being made in human likeness. And being found in appearance as a man, he humbled himself and became obedient to death-- even death on a cross! Therefore God exalted him to the highest place and gave him the name that is above every name, that at the name of Jesus every knee should bow, in heaven and on earth and under the earth, and every tongue confess that Jesus Christ is Lord, to the glory of God the Father." Philippians 2:5-11

In the upside down world of faith, it is a "great paradox in Christianity that it makes humility the avenue to glory" according to the *Easton's Bible Dictionary*.

In the Air Force I worked hard to become upwardly mobile, and it resulted in eventual promotion to Colonel before I retired. But, working at the church is a totally new paradigm. Now I don't have to work for promotion, because I am already upwardly mobile (heaven bound), even while I'm getting make-up for Bob Russell.

Odd that applying for Medicare would make me sick

I knew this day would come, I just didn't expect it to arrive so soon. Not long ago I signed up for Medicare. In case you missed the memo or slept through high school social studies, that meant I would soon be 65 years old.

The letter I received advised me that I had three months to contact Social Security to enroll. I wondered why I needed 90 days to sign up until I began navigating through the phone prompts. "Press one for English, two for Spanish, three for Swahili, etc." After what seemed like days, I finally arrived at a voice recorded message that first apologized for the long wait and then advised me to call back "later" since no one was available to help me. Perhaps they failed to consider that at 64+ years, I don't have that much "later" left.

I had flashbacks to my days in the military contending with the largest bureaucracy in the world. I could feel my blood pressure rising in response to the frustration, I knew gastric acid was eating away at the lining of my stomach and I feared a heart attack or stroke was imminent. I thought of the irony of the situation: Medicare was making me sick.

When I finally got through to a living person, I talked to a very nice young man (actually I have no idea of his age but when you're applying for Medicare you just assume everyone is younger than you) who walked me through the process and assured me my Medicare Card would be forwarded soon. I knew I would be the envy of everyone in my circle of friends until it occurred to me that most of my friends were either dead, in the nursing home or have had their cards for years. Growing old is the pits.

My wife, Nancy, attempts to console me by cheerily repeating the old cliché, "You're only as old as you feel." "Right," I respond dryly "that's what really worries me."

Now there is *some* good news in all the old age talk. We're living longer today. At the turn of last century, the life expectancy of an American was 50 years old. If I had been living back then, I would have died 14 years ago. (I know that's a confusing sentence, but you know what I mean.) With today's life expectancy of 77.6 years, I figure I may have 12.7 years or so to go. The real question is, "what am I going to with that precious time?"

I have tried to stay in shape to enhance the quality and length of my life by eating the right foods and getting exercising regularly. Experts suggest that for every mile you jog, you add one minute to your life. Now, it has occurred to me that my regular exercise over the past 40 years will allow me to spend an additional 5 months in a nursing home at $5000 per month. I don't think Medicare will cover this.

The Bible is helpful in sorting out my mixed emotions about my advancing years. Consider what it says about old age. First, it chronicles the lives of some pretty old people. For example as I have noted in other articles, Enoch lived 365 years before God took him, Noah was 950 years old and we all know about Methuselah who lived to be 969 years old. And that's without Medicare! That's a lot of senior citizens discounts and AARP dues.

What else does the Bible teach about old age? The elderly are to be revered for their wisdom. "Rise in the presence of the aged, show respect for the elderly and revere your God. I am the LORD." Leviticus 19:32 Or as Job said in chapter 12: "Is not wisdom found among the aged? Does not long life bring understanding?" Actually, I haven't noticed any additional reverence since I received my first copy of *Modern Maturity*.

As I read the Scriptures, the main teaching of the Bible is that the length of life is far less important than what we do with the life God has given us. Sure, we all want to live a long and productive life; but at the very best life is short, and unfortunately you don't fully appreciate that until you wake up one morning and have to apply for Medicare. As James put it: "What is your life? You are a mist that appears for a little while and then vanishes." James 4:14

What is your life? How do you regard your brief time on earth? Is it primarily an experience we want to maximize, "go for the gusto," be all you can be, make your Medicare payments and live a long time? Or rather is this life primarily a preparation for the next one, which lasts forever...if you are a Christian.

Nancy's MS

I was watching "Law and Order" last week and one of the main characters, Ray, was having to leave his job to take care of his wife who had multiple sclerosis. I remember when I first heard the words "Multiple Sclerosis" used in conjunction with my wife, Nancy. The words sounded hideous and ominous. At the time, I was 23 and Nancy and I were living in Ohio. Nancy was pregnant with our first child and we had returned home to visit our parents. While at home Nancy's mother suggested she visit her family doctor. Nancy complied and I drove her to her appointment remaining in the waiting room until Dr. Murphy summoned me for a private conversation.

He explained that Nancy had had some abnormal neurological symptoms when she was 19, and he thought she might have MS. Nancy was unaware of this diagnosis, but Dr. Murphy wanted me to know in case there were complications with the pregnancy. I cannot adequately express my feelings following my meeting with Nancy's doctor. I had visions of wheel chairs, canes and nursing homes. It didn't seem fair. We were so young and just beginning our lives together; we were excited about starting a family. Why, God?

Why are You allowing this to happen to us? It was years later before I learned the answer to this haunting question.

When I learned Nancy might have MS I had to consult a medical dictionary for details. I learned that Multiple Sclerosis is a chronic, often disabling disease of the central nervous system. No one knows what causes MS but it is more common in the northern regions of the world.

Symptoms may be mild such as numbness in the limbs and minor vision problems or severe involving paralysis, loss of vision and in rare cases death. Most people with MS are diagnosed between the ages of 20 and 40 but the unpredictable physical and emotional effects can be life long. Nationwide, there are an estimated 250,000 to 350,000 people with MS. There is no known cure but Nancy has been taking Beta Interferon injections every other night for the past 17 years. This very expensive drug seems to suppress major exacerbations, although we endured a six-month long ordeal in 2011.

Shortly after I was told of Nancy's MS, there came a time to tell Nancy. Still, given the nature of the disease, a definitive diagnosis was elusive. One of the frustrations is that she appears normal to others, even to some doctors. For years, Nancy had recurring periods of extreme fatigue, blurred vision, numbness in left side and some occasional problems walking.

Every 6-8 years she had a major exacerbation, which left her essentially, bed ridden for one to three months. It was during one of these exacerbations in 1988 that we finally got a definitive diagnosis due to the development of the MRI. At the time of her attack, we were in the process of moving from Soesterberg, Holland to Bitburg, Germany. I thank God for our Air Force family who helped us move. At one time I had two kids in Holland, one with me in Bitburg, Germany and Nancy in a hospital in Ramstein Germany. The moving van was somewhere in between. But we got the job done and Nancy eventually got back on her feet.

Nancy has always been getting the job done despite her illness. She seldom complains and never asks "why me?" She raised three kids despite her disease and the rigors of 22 moves in 28 years. She was the perfect, though sometimes absent, Air Force officer's wife often going to obligatory functions when she didn't feel like it.

I recall one episode in particular. It was September 1978. I had left Virginia for Holland and Nancy and the kids were to join me as soon as I could find housing. For three weeks I searched for housing, met new friends, flew jets and had a pretty good time while she closed on the house, took care of a million details associated with the move, got the kids out of school, etc.

Then she got on a plane with three kids, ages 10, 8 and 5 and flew to Europe. Unfortunately, the weather in Holland was so bad no one could land, so she had to spend 28 hours in London's Heathrow Airport lobby before flying to Brussels and being bused to Holland. This ordeal would have been a strain on a healthy person. When I met her at the bus I was in agony for her. I felt guilty that I had put her though all this.

I am sharing the story of Nancy's MS with you for a couple of reasons. First, I want everyone to know how proud I am of Nancy, and what she's been able to accomplish though stricken with a chronic and debilitating disease. She has used her illness to glorify God and share her faith. One way she's done that is by organizing the Southeast MS Support Group some years ago. This group provided encouragement to fellow sufferers and their families, brought in experts to recommend therapies and provided a system of mutual support. We have many friends today because of this group.

I also want to let you know that we have discovered the scriptural truth that we really can give thanks to God even in difficult circumstances. Nancy's illness has drawn us closer together, and we're grateful she has a relatively mild case of MS. We certainly have learned to appreciate the times when she feels normal. We also better understand now that God can use suffering to accomplish His purposes, to bring Him glory, and to spread the Gospel.

> *"Be joyful always; pray continually; give thanks in all circumstances, for this is God's will for you in Christ Jesus." 1 Thessalonians 5:16-18*

My MS diagnosis. I didn't know it was spread that way.

Earlier I wrote about Nancy's long time battle with MS, a chronic debilitating disease of the central nervous system. I am so proud of the way she supported me and my career, raised three kids and glorified God while contending with this dreaded disease. She's my hero.

Our 46-year battle with MS took a humorous twist in 1994. At the time, I was a professor at Air War College anticipating retirement in a couple of years. I awoke one morning so dizzy I couldn't walk. Nancy recognized that was strange conduct even for me and took me to the Base hospital where I saw the neurologist, a humorless man who bored an eerie resemblance to Dr. Kevorkian, the late champion of physician assisted suicide. "Dr. Kevorkian" poked and probed and ordered a series of tests including an MRI to determine what was causing my dizziness, and I went home to await the results.

At 7 a.m. the next morning my doctor called and said he needed to see me ASAP. I swallowed hard. The urgency suggested a bad report, and my imagination ran wild as Nancy drove me to the hospital. I was certain I had an inoperable brain tumor or worse.

The nurse ushered us into the doctor's office. He had a serious look on his face and peered over the MRI report, his half glasses dangling precariously close to the end of his nose. "Colonel Waddell," he began ominously "I have some bad news for you... (It seemed like several hours passed before he completed the sentence.)...the MRI reveals that you probably have Multiple Sclerosis."

He paused momentarily waiting for my response. I looked at Nancy and she looked at me and then we both started laughing. Actually, this was not the reaction my doctor expected. "I didn't know it was spread that way," I responded laughing out loud. After regaining my composure, I explained that Nancy had MS, and we were just struck by the irony of the diagnosis.

Soon thereafter, Nancy and I were medevaced to Andrews AFB to meet with the Air Force's foremost authority on MS. I carried Nancy's MS medication that had to be stored in a small cooler to protect it from the heat. Throughout the flight a young lady travelling with us kept glancing in our direction with a look of curiosity on her face. When we arrived at our destination, she requested to ask the Colonel a personal question. She looked at me and at the cooler and then asked, "Is there an organ in the cooler?" In light of the fact that we were on an apparently urgent medevac mission, it seemed like a logical question. I wish I had been quick enough to say, "Yes, I have to have a heart replacement, and I must transport my own donor heart due to budget cutbacks."

During the next two days, I was poked and probed and interrogated, again. The examination included a spinal tap. That's where a very long needle is stuck in your spinal column to extract spinal fluid. Naturally I was a little apprehensive about another human being inserting a sharp object into my spinal column, and the word "paraplegic" kept ringing in my ears. My apprehension increased when I met the doctor who was going to perform the procedure; he was so young I doubted that he had started shaving yet. I didn't have the courage to ask him how many "lumbar punctures" he had previously performed. After the procedure I learned I was his third patient, a reality that made me really nervous retroactively.

The spinal tap was negative, and the results of the exam inconclusive. Later a new neurologist reported to my hospital at Maxwell AFB, conducted some additional tests and determined that I had "thick" blood. I'm sure there's a more technical, Latin name for my condition, but according to her I had had a small stroke that caused my dizziness and presented itself as MS symptoms. Actually I wasn't sure a stroke was preferable to MS but I didn't get vote in the matter. In any event, an aspirin a day has kept me symptom free since then.

What did I learn from all of this? Though not without its weaknesses and inequalities, we benefit from a wonderful medical care system in America. We are so blessed. Our medical personnel can cure diseases, reduce pain and suffering, help us live longer, more healthy lives. But in the end, good medical care only forestalls the inevitable, because we all will eventually die. That's why we need the "Great Physician," Jesus.

During his public ministry here on earth (for example, Matthew 4:23-25), Jesus healed many people including lepers, the blind and deaf, the lame and others suffering from debilitating diseases (perhaps even multiple sclerosis). Yet, as awesome as these miracles were, they only provided temporary relief, because in the end we all die.

As the "Great Physician" Jesus provides complete healing in the form of eternal life to all who place their faith in Him. "For God so loved the world that He gave his one and only Son, that whosoever believes in Him should not perish but have eternal life" free from sickness, disease and pain forever.

Shopping at the speed of light can be hazardous to your wealth

Welcome to the new year. It's time again for those well-intentioned but often short-lived New Year's resolutions. What's yours this year? Lose 10 pounds? Get out of debt? Give up (choose one) drinking, smoking, gossip, or Red Man chewing tobacco.

I've made a new type of resolution this year. This year I made one for Nancy. I resolved for Nancy that she would not do anymore on-line shopping. This extreme action is all the more remarkable since Nancy is about as computer illiterate as a girl can get short of not being able to use a microwave. The incident that prompted me to take this drastic action took place in Tallahassee while we were visiting the kids over Thanksgiving.

It was Saturday and the guys were watching the FSU-Florida football game oblivious to anything outside the activities taking place on the TV screen. Meanwhile, unbeknownst to the guys, the ladies were in the kitchen gathered around my laptop computer.

Midway through the second quarter, my daughter-in-law Rae, yelled in from the kitchen: "Hey, grumppa, what's the password for your AOL account." "Without thinking," I said "it's "XXXXXX." (I may have been stupid enough to give it to Rae but I'm not giving it to you!) Later, Nancy came in during a particularly tense part of the game and asked for my credit card. I handed it to her without thinking.

At half time I went into the kitchen to get a coke and came upon my worst nightmare. My wife and two daughters-in-law were gathered around the computer, my credit cards spread out on the kitchen table, my password already entered and they were shopping. All three of the ladies were visibly drooling. What terrified me was that their shopping wasn't confined to a store or the Mall. They were shopping the infinite array of stores on the Internet. I thought nothing was faster than Nancy trying to beat a fellow shopper to the 50% off table, but the girls were shopping at the speed of light.

I was pretty sure my credit card bill was going to approximate the national debt when the bills started rolling in, and I was convinced that no man could top my story. That was before I shared my story with Charles McKibben, who along with his wife Jo are faithful volunteers in our New Member Ministry. Last month my team took some of our volunteers out to lunch, and I was relating my travails to Charles as Jo sat next to him. By Jo's own admission she has the spiritual gift of shopping. Actually, even after teaching in our spiritual gifts program for several years I've never heard about this gift in the Bible. I must have missed something.

Charles related the story about the time he got a call from his credit card company's fraud division about a large number of suspicious purchases being made around the country on his credit card. "Well, it must be a thief," Charles responded "because my wife is home sick in bed." His suspicions were aroused when he attempted to call home to check out the problem and the phone was busy. When he finally got through, Jo confessed that she was catalog shopping over the phone. "But I thought you were sick," Charles protested.

The one with the spiritual gift of shopping responded, "I'm not so sick I couldn't shop." You really have to admire such commitment.

Charles then related an incident, which occurred at a shoe outlet store in Indiana. The shopping was almost completed and Charles was holding a place in the checkout line, while Jo and a friend were making last minute purchases. When all three rendezvoused to pay for the merchandise, Jo's friend was admiring one of Jo's purchases. "Oh yes," bragged Jo, "that's a $50 pair of shoes I got for $5." Her friend responded with a mixture of envy and appreciation only truly compulsive shoppers understand, "That's a great buy!" Jo nodded in agreement but then said... "I just wish they were the right size." (!)

So if you have any compulsive on-line shoppers, catalog shoppers or just garden-variety mall-hopping shoppers in your house, this could be the year you can resolve that they shop less.

However, if you haven't come up with a new year's resolution for yourself yet, let me suggest one---If you haven't already done so, start a daily quiet time with God. In 1990, I resolved to start a daily quiet time with God. Initially I was motivated by a sense of duty, but now I look forward to my time alone with God. A daily quiet time is essential, I think, for us to grow as disciples of Christ.

Successful devotions, I think, need to take place at a regular time and a regular place. For me that is early in the morning on the kitchen table before the crush of daily activities distract me. I usually spend some time in God's word making notes in the margin of my Bible as I read or I follow a published devotional such as Oswald Chambers, *Our Daily Bread* or the one published in the A section of the *Outlook*. I then pray for a while. The most practical book on prayer I have read is *Too Busy Not To Pray*, by Bill Hybels. I keep a list of prayer needs in my Bible for reference.

You can have your spouse purchase any of these items on line if you want...but I don't recommend it.

Sacrificial giving
without the sacrifice

Periodically our preachers talk about stewardship at the beginning of the year. Since Jesus talked so often about money, this is always an appropriate and convicting topic, and it got me to thinking about a situation involving my personal stewardship some years ago.

The event centered around the "Making Room For More" (MRFM) capital campaign when our church was trying to raise money to expand several areas on our campus. Wanting to help, Nancy and I agreed to host a MRFM evening of prayer at our house and considered how we could give sacrificially.

In anticipation of strangers coming to our house, Nancy worried that the interior of the house needed to be painted. I told her we needed to save the money for the MRFM campaign. Besides, at the time it had only been seven years since we moved in to our new quarters, so it couldn't possibly need painting. Not only that but, I like off white- - -it's my favorite color. How about I just touch up in a few places, I countered hoping to save the money a new paint job would require.

So, I found the original cans of paint left by the painter in 1996. They were rusted shut now. I pried one of them open and almost lost my lunch when I eyed the contents. It looked for all the world like a petri dish culture of some exotic bacteria grown in a research laboratory in Maryland. The gooey, discolored mess resembled a collection of pond scum more than an interior, latex, semi-gloss paint. Ugh!

Having committed myself to touching up, now I had to buy some new paint. I carefully wrote down the paint name and code and looked in the phone book for a paint store where I could find the exact match to the original color which was called "Parisian Foam," or some such. The helpful gentleman who waited on me performed a computer search for the right formula and spent quite a bit of time mixing and matching. Still, $25 seemed like a lot for a gallon of paint. I also picked up some new paint brushes that, judging by the price, must have been made from mink hair bristles.

So my day off was spent touching up our living room, dining room and kitchen with Parisian Foam. Exhausted from all the work, I took a nap while the paint dried and awoke to inspect my work. I was shocked. The living room looked like a set of desert camouflaged BDUs with small splotches and dabs of new Parisian Foam, significantly darker than the original. Whoops. The older Parisian Foam had been bleached by seven years exposure to the light.

So the remainder of my day off was spent completely painting large portions of our living room interior. And it was all a waste. Nancy is now more committed than ever to repainting the interior of our house. And she's not as fond of Parisian Foam as I and wants a more colorful décor. I think she's looking at chartreuse and periwinkle or something like that.

Then I had a brilliant idea. I proposed that we forgo painting our house and use the money saved as our sacrificial giving for MRFM. What a stratagem! I could sacrifice for the building campaign and not have to paint the house. Win-win to my way of thinking; kind of like sacrificial giving without the sacrifice. I was crushed when Nancy vetoed the idea lecturing me that that wasn't what God expected. I guess I'll have to find a more tangible way to sacrifice in a significant way.

But that's hard. After all I am just a retired civil servant turned minister. That's not the traditional path to becoming a millionaire. I'm also married to a woman with extravagant tastes and an affinity for exotic dogs, anniversary rings, jet setting life style, and multiple, spoiled grandchildren.

While my MRFM gift wasn't all that much in absolute terms, it did represent a big improvement from a stewardship perspective as compared to the Don Waddell of 25 years ago. As a young adult I was kind of stingy. We bought more house than we could afford and wanted to save for kids' college and our retirement. I returned some of what God blessed me with, but mostly it came from what was left over. As we became more involved with the work the church was doing, the giving increased. Eventually we began to tithe, and we have been blessed "more than we could ask or imagine" ever since.

Over time, we really just became content with less as our focus shifted more to the eternal than on the temporal. For us, God has proven the truth of Malachi 3:8-12 where He says in verse ten, 'Bring the whole tithe into the storehouse, that there may be food in my house. Test me in this,' says the LORD Almighty, 'and see if I will not throw open the floodgates of heaven and pour out so much blessing that there will not be room enough to store it.'

My most expensive Valentine's Day ever

In our 35 years of marital bliss (did you ever notice how similar the word "marital" and "martial" are?) Nancy and I have never been very ceremonial, and recently we've gotten to the point that we seldom exchange gifts on the major holidays. We're more inclined to buy something special on random occasions throughout the year than go overboard on a holiday or one of the Hallmark-fabricated special days. It's not that we don't care for each other, it's just that my needs are very modest and Nancy is pretty much showered with gifts 365 days a year. I mean, just living with me has to be swell thing.

We planned to let Valentine's Day pass without fanfare again this year. However, I discovered too late, that that can be a very expensive option. I should have listened closer to Bob, who in a recent sermon told us that we shouldn't believe our wives when they tell us they don't want anything for Valentine's Day. After church, I pressed Nancy for what I could get her that would satisfy her every romantic desire. "A normal sized husband," she responded with a curious look that left me wondering whether she was serious or not.

"No really," I probed, "What do you want?" Bob said you are breaking the 9th commandment if you say "nothing."

In the past I've done a considerable amount of Valentine's Day shopping at Cracker Barrel. I realize it's not as romantic as a candlelight dinner for two at some secluded hideaway or buying some provocative lingerie from Victoria Secrets. But, if you're a minister at Southeast you spend much of your adult life eating at Cracker Barrel, so, it's convenient for me to catch up on my Valentine's Day shopping there.

I found some cool gifts for my bride. First there was the Whistling Monkey, what every girl wants. The high tech stuffed primate is equipped with a motion detector enabling it to whistle a good catcall every time Nancy passed by. That's got to make a girl's heart beat faster. Unfortunately, the monkey also whistled when the dog or cat went by as well. Then there was the Singing Posey that sang a computer-generated ditty as the flowers danced merrily to a Bosanova beat. That was special.

I don't know if Nancy appreciated the gifts I acquired at Cracker Barrel exactly, but I was able to write a couple of *Outlook* articles based on the experiences. But what should I get my bride this year? Surely there must be something. "OK," she responded reluctantly, "I either need a new watch or new batteries for the ones I have." That sounded doable, and she went to the bedroom and returned with not one, but 4 dead watches. I suggested that it might be easier to buy a new watch than replace the batteries, but we decided that a fifth watch wasn't the answer. The symbolism of this was poignant. My love was timeless, my feelings for her were energizing, my personality electric, I surmised. "I still need the batteries," Nancy said crossly.

Normally, I'm not a procrastinator, but I waited until Valentine's Day to go by a local department store and acquire new batteries for my honey. That took more time that I antic-ipated so while I waited for the saleswoman to locate and install the batteries, I wandered around the store and yes, I bought some stuff I wouldn't have purchased otherwise. Nevertheless, I was really proud of myself as I left the store with an operational watch, confident I'd be receiving many votes for "Husband of the Year."

On the way home, however, I recalled that one of our receptionists had gotten some nice flowers delivered to her at church. I thought I could go the extra mile for my sweetheart without going out of my way (if you know what I mean), so I drove about 5280 feet out of my way to the local florist. I don't know what possessed me to do this. It was 3:00 o'clock in the afternoon on Valentine's Day, and I was in a florist! I need to have my head examined. Every man in Louisville was in the florist doing exactly the same thing I was doing. I waited long enough to determine I was probably going to spend the balance of my life on earth waiting to be served. I also noticed that most arrangements were in the $60 class.

So I snuck out and drove to a grocery store nearby where I knew I could get some flowers quickly and for a whole lot less than $60. While they weren't as expensive as the others, I felt certain they would last at least until I got home. I found some nice tulips. Having lived in Holland for four years, Nancy likes tulips so I grabbed some red ones. I'm sure now I had "Husband of the Year" in the bag.

Unfortunately, I also bought some other things while I was in the store. I was standing in line with several other men with flowers to purchase for their Valentine. Apparently they too had tired of waiting at the local florist. I was moving forward in the line and could almost see the cashier in the distance when a gentleman behind me squeezed a stuffed animal he was purchasing for his sweetheart, and it played a pretty, little ditty. Reluctantly, I looked over my shoulder and sighed deeply. I was afraid of that. It was a stuffed Bichon Frise that looked exactly like our dog. I knew now my arrival home would be further delayed and my Visa bill was approaching the national debt.

What started out as an inexpensive Valentine's Day of watch batteries, ended up costing me a King's (or perhaps Queen's) ransom. Next year I'm going to buy Nancy a trip to Hawaii. I think it might be cheaper.

I have the eyes of an eagle, but...

"**D**uck, break right!" my wingman screamed over the radio referring to me by my tactical call sign, "you've got a bandit at your six o'clock." "Roger," I replied calmly, "Tally ho. I am engaged on the bandit, visual on you." So went many mock air-to-air battles during my 25 years as a fighter pilot.

As I reflect on my years of flying and fighting, I am reminded how important good vision is to the fighter pilot. Good vision is, indeed, a matter of life and death in combat.

Not long after I quit flying, my vision began to deteriorate due, I am told, to my advancing years. You see as you age your lens becomes less and less elastic and as a consequence it becomes increasingly difficult to focus on things close to your eyes. I first noticed this when I had to hold what I was reading further and further away until my arms weren't long enough. I joked that I still had the eyes of an eagle, but unfortunately I had the arms of a penguin. I have recently learned that the word for this is presbyopia, which sounds like a sect of Calvinism.

About age forty-five I had to get glasses and this was a real blow to my ego. I was growing old. Initially, I only wore them when reading, but I keep misplacing my glasses so I bought about a dozen of the drugstore readers of varying magnifications and had at least one pair in each room of our house. As I aged, I progressively purchased glasses with greater magnification. Then came bifocals. Then trifocals. Then glasses with progressive lens. These spectacles have no lines and a broader range of magnifications, but have a narrow field of view and can make you dizzy until you get used to them. Bottomline: Glasses are a nuisance.

Then one Sunday I saw Bob Russell stand up in the pulpit without wearing his customary glasses and thought "it's a miracle." I later learned that he had had Lasik surgery performed on his eyes and I decided I wanted that too. Cost was a factor but the clinic I attended had a generous clergy discount, which made the procedure a possibility financially. As I reported in for my eye exam, I thought of the sign over the door of one optometrist's office. "If you don't see what you're looking for, you've come to the right place."

Here's how Lasik works. The surgeon cuts the membrane covering the eye and peels it back. A laser then reshapes the lens to correct the vision as desired. In my case, we corrected the left eye, my non-dominate eye to be 20/20 for close vision, reading, and left the right eye alone since it was almost 20/20 for far vision. The procedure itself took about two minutes and was completely painless.

This was amazing to me for two reasons. One, the technical sophistication of laser technology is mind-boggling. The laser beam accurately reshapes the lens and even compensates for eye movement during the surgery. Two, one eye is adjusted to see near while the other is optimized for distance vision, a procedure called monovision. One eye sees perfectly near, the other eye sees perfectly far and your brain figures all that out by itself.

I'm pretty sure I don't understand how this is possible but I am equally sure God did a pretty good job when he designed our eye. For me there was a considerable adjustment time until my brain figured this monovision thing out (I am told some brains are slower than others.) During the adjustment time, I would occasionally close one eye so I could see better. Thinking I was getting fresh by winking at her, one lady almost slapped me while I was trying to clear up my vision. At any rate, I like being without my glasses and being able to see again.

Then it occurred to me. Good vision, spiritually speaking, is also a matter of life and death---eternal life and death. About our spiritual vision, the Bible makes at least three points:

One, the truth is there for all to see but we must choose to see, to believe. Seeing the truth is a voluntary act. In Matthew 13:14-17 we read: "In them is fulfilled the prophecy of Isaiah: "'You will be ever hearing but never understanding; you will be ever seeing but never perceiving... they have closed their eyes. Otherwise they might see with their eyes, hear with their ears, understand with their hearts and turn, and I would heal them.' But blessed are your eyes because they see, and your ears because they hear."

The evidence of God's existence, His love and His plan for us is readily apparent if we will open our eyes. Unfortunately, many in our culture have allowed themselves to become spiritually blind. Spiritual Lasik surgery was available to them but they declined. As Paul wrote in Romans 1:20 "For since the creation of the world God's invisible qualities—his eternal power and divine nature— have been clearly seen, being understood from what has been made, so that people are without excuse."

Two, we can avoid spiritual blindness by focusing on the right things. Jesus taught us that spiritual vision is more important than physical vision. He said: Luke 11:34 "Your eye is the lamp of your body. When your eyes are good, your whole body also is full of light. But when they are bad, your body also is full of darkness." Paul counseled the church in

Corinth to fix their eyes not on what is seen, but on what is unseen. "For what is seen is temporary, but what is unseen is eternal." 2 Corinthians 2:18 "We must fix our eyes on Jesus the author and perfecter of our faith..." Hebrews 12:2. And we learn of him through God's word, "a light unto my feet a lamp unto my path." Psalm 119:105

Finally, since our spiritual vision as followers of Christ is good enough to see the truth, it is our duty to help those with spiritual vision problems. Acts 26:17-18: "I will rescue you from your own people and from the Gentiles. I am sending you to them to open their eyes and turn them from darkness to light and from the power of Satan to God, so that they may receive forgiveness of sins and a place among those who are sanctified by faith in me."

My perfect vision enabled me to survive many close calls while flying, since I was able to accurately assess the environment around me and avoid potential dangers. Our spiritual eyesight provides the same advantage in our daily lives provided we focus on the right things.

House cleaning tips for slobs

Mark 13:32 "No one knows about that day or hour, not even the angels in heaven, nor the Son, but only the Father. 33 Be on guard! Be alert! You do not know when that time will come."

I was visiting my parents recently while Nancy was staying with our kids and grandkids in Tallahassee. "Isn't Nancy coming home today?" mom asked. "Oh, no, it's next Saturday. She always stays two weeks," I responded nonchalantly. "Are you sure?" Mom repeated.

My confidence waning, I called Nancy's cell phone. "Hello" she said cheerily. "Where are you?" I queried, my voice quivering now. "I'm just turning off I-10 and heading north toward Montgomery. I'll be home this evening." My heart sank. "Please drive very, very slowly," I pleaded. I was less concerned about her safety than my survival. You see I was expecting her the following Saturday, and the house was not in "inspection order" at the time.

I rushed home from my parents to see how much cleaning I could get done before Nancy pulled into our drive. I surveyed the interior of our house, the result of seven days of "baching" it with Zac, our not-too-tidy Bichon Frise. It was not a pretty sight. His toys were scattered all over the house.

To be honest, my toys were also scattered all over the house. Fast food wrappers littered the kitchen table. The trash overflowed. The sink was full of dishes stacked higher than my head. That would be more impressive if I was taller, but you get my point.

As I considered the challenge before me I recalled a sign posted in the church break room adjacent to the microwave and community refrigerator that said: "If cleanliness is next to godliness, how close are you?" The Scripture Psalm 103:12 came to my mind, "as far as the east is from the west." So I immediately set about to clean the house or at least create the illusion of cleanliness.

I knew I was going to be in big trouble if Nancy returned home to a dirty house. It's not that she's unreasonable or overly demanding, but due to her MS I don't want her to come home to a lot of work. Besides, she always comes home exhausted. Everyone is sympathetic with Nancy because she has MS, but I could use a little sympathy too. I'm the one who has to say home and work while she has all the fun. I'm the one who has to work overtime to support her in the extravagant lifestyle to which she has grown accustomed. I'm the one who has to come home every day at noon to take the dog out when she's gone.

This was such an inconvenience, so I tried to see how long Zac could go between potty breaks. My theory was that about six to eight hours elapsed between going to bed at night and getting up in the morning, so I figured that he should be able to hold it at least that long while I was working overtime saving souls at church.

As luck would have it, the carpet square we wipe our feet on as we enter the utility room from the garage lies exactly where Zac's papers were placed when he was paper trained as a puppy. I guess I should have seen it coming, but when I returned from work the carpet squished when I stepped on it. Unfortunately, I had already taken my shoes off. At that moment, I knew then that his endurance was something less than I had estimated. Oh, joy. Another mess to clean up.

Now mind you, I'm not without experience cleaning. At an early age mom convinced me of the virtue of cleanliness. "Clean this room or you're grounded forever" she was fond of saying. The Air Force taught me the finer points of cleaning the latrine floor with a toothbrush. But today, I had a lot of work to do and not much time to do it. So just in case you men find yourself in a similar situation, I'd like to share a couple of house cleaning shortcuts sure to put you in the running for "Husband of the Year."

Tip 1 - Never vacuum under anything. It's really quite unnecessary, and it saves lots of time and energy. Moving furniture only stirs up a lot of dust.

Tip 2 – Go for superficial cleanliness. You'll not get extra points for a clean toilet bowl if the wastebaskets are overflowing.

Tip 3 - A woman's primary sensory organ is her nose and the smell of Lysol alone is enough to create the illusion of cleanliness regardless of the actual tidiness. So, scatter significant quantities of Lysol around the house especially around the entryways.

By the time Nancy had arrived that evening, the house at least gave the appearance of being clean. Her reaction, however, was unexpected. "Did someone spill the Lysol?" she asked as she entered through the utility room and rubbed her eyes that were beginning to water due to the pungent odor of the concentrated cleaner. "Oh no," I responded in part truthfully, "I've just been cleaning." Then I heard a squishing sound as she stepped onto the carpet square in the utility room. Oops. Maybe going for superficial wasn't such a good idea. I wished then I had been better prepared for her return.

The spiritual application here is pretty obvious, I think. We don't know when Christ will return, so we need to keep our spiritual house in order 24/7. And there are no spiritual shortcuts to being ready for his return. Mark 13:35 "Therefore keep watch because you do not know when the owner of the house will come back--whether in the evening, or at midnight, or when the rooster crows, or at dawn."

Returning to Vietnam
30 years later: Two granddads compare "war stories"

His name was Nguyen, a 65-year-old construction supervisor. He and his crew were building a new sewer system for a small town east of Hanoi. My group and I were there shopping for pottery, as tourists are wont to do, but our real purpose was to explore the possibility of launching a missions outpost in Vietnam.

Three of us had served in Vietnam in the 60s and 70s and while each had our own motive, I was prompted to return out of curiosity and perhaps to address some lingering unresolved issues of my wartime experience. Perhaps Nguyen could help, I thought, as we labored to have a conversation between a vital, but aging Vietnamese veteran and a middle aged American fighter pilot turned minister.

For me there were lingering anxieties about my wartime experience. I had never been comfortable with the notion of taking the life of another human being, even in combat. Yes, I know I was fighting armed combatants who were shooting back at me. Still it seemed so barbaric and inhumane no matter how you looked at it. General Sherman's observation that "War is hell" didn't quite seem to fully address this intensely personal issue.

Even before WWJD became a fashionable question to ask, I wondered what Jesus would do if he were drafted in 1967 and subsequently found himself in Vietnam. Another unresolved issue was that the war had gone badly---we lost. As I read about the war and later taught the strategy and history of the Vietnam War to Senior Officers at Air War College, I came to believe that our involvement in Southeast Asia had been a tragic mistake.

Previously I had defended our involvement in Vietnam and energetically argued that military action was needed to stem the spread of communism as if a political philosophy were going to suppress the culture and nationalism of a proud people who had been invaded, occupied and abused by so called civilized nations for hundreds of years. If I was wrong about the war being justified, I felt stupid and betrayed. Worse yet, if I were wrong it undermined my whole rationale for fighting and killing.

The duty I wanted to perform on behalf of my country seemed less noble, maybe wrong. 58,000 Americans were killed; countless others died. For what purpose? Others had opposed the war as morally wrong. I had ridiculed their opposition. Now it seemed they were right. What should I do to atone for my mistake? What should my penitence be? So good people on both sides of the conflict died for no good reason it would seem, and I took part as a young ambitious airman thinking more of my career than the moral suppositions upon which I would make my decisions.

During the trip to Southeast Asia, my soul searching began in earnest as we made our approach into Vietnam from Thailand. The Vietnamese airline followed roughly the same route of flight as I had on some of my missions in 1972 when US forces were attacking North Vietnam on a daily basis. The terrain below was familiar---rugged, robust jungle---but on this flight I did not see the incessant flashes from the muzzles of anti-aircraft guns which sparkled from the ground below or the burst of FLAK that often produced dreary, deadly clouds of black. Absent was the occasional contrail of a SAM making its way toward an American airplane.

As we touched down and taxied in, I waited for a personal reaction: Nostalgia? Anger? Remorse? I felt nothing in particular. It's possible that the job of an airman is too abstract, too impersonal to evoke an emotional reaction 30 years later. Unlike my army counter parts who got to see the face of death up close and personal, death for the airman is abstract and almost unemotional for the most part. A bomb you released would explode a mile below and people would die, or a fireball would suddenly appear where an aircraft piloted by a friend was a moment or two before. Or after landing, the dreaded letters "MIA" (missing in action) would appear next to the name on the scheduling board.

No, war for the airman was less about dying and more about pushing buttons, less about blood and screams of agony than it is a deadly, exciting contest decided from a distance. It is about technique. It's distant and impersonal except perhaps in the mind of the pilot. There war can be very personal, especially when it is allowed to fester for 30 years.

To be honest I was disappointed at my lack of emotion. I had hoped for a dramatic feeling, a catharsis perhaps. None came.

As we stepped out of the plane and on to the tarmac at the Hanoi airport, I had my first genuine taste of nostalgia---it was the thick, moist oppressive heat. I had almost forgotten about the heat and humidity. The enveloping humidity was punctuated by the familiar, nasal chatter of the Vietnamese people that evoked another emotional response. It wasn't an unpleasant emotion exactly, but it did resurrect an angst, an uneasy malaise that I couldn't put my finger on.

The emotion conjured up mixed feelings of excitement and dread; adventure on the one hand; despair on the other; the excitement of flying in combat, frustrated by one year of separation from my family. Up to this point in my life, my resentment of the Vietnam War was largely confined to the fact that it robbed me of one year, about 1/20th of my opportunity to be a dad to my kids as they grew up. My relationship with my wife had been relegated to daily, sometimes painful letters or late night, HAM operator assisted phone calls that were more frustrating than satisfying. All this made the war very personal and painful.

But now, 30 years later I was walking in Vietnam International Airport---this used to be a target. I was surrounded by thousands of Vietnamese people---they used to be my enemy. I reflected on my activities 30 years ago and they seemed too distant, remote, irrelevant.

The Vietnamese, or "gooks" as we used to call them were not overly friendly but they were polite and respectful. There were hundreds working hard to extend the airport runway in a massive project to upgrade the facility. I imagine that runway repair must have been a familiar scene following air attacks in 1972. The Vietnamese were legendary for being able to repair runways over night following our bombing attacks. Now I was seeing their industriousness first hand. These were not the aimless people I once believed them to be.

In the terminal, service personnel were engaging, polite and friendly. As we drove in the countryside heading for our hotel, it was inundated with people diligently tending to the ubiquitous rice fields. When I went to run at 6 a.m. the next morning I was amazed to find the streets abuzz with activity. Shops were already open, families were walking together, playing badminton together, sweeping sidewalks or scurrying around on mopeds overloaded with people or produce. These were not the lazy, no-account people we had looked upon condescendingly in 1972.

Then came my second emotional reaction. I liked these people. They were not my enemy and perhaps they never had been. During the war we invented dehumanizing names to make it easier to drop napalm on them and strafe their positions. We called them "gooks" and "zips." We repeated stories of atrocities and unfair treatment. It's always easier to kill someone you hate. But in reality, I couldn't hate them in 1972, and I was starting to admire them in 2002.

Then I met Nguyen my new Vietnamese friend just outside a pottery shop owned by his cousin. He was a slight man, short even by my standards. He sought me out and asked in broken, uncertain English. "Where from?" "United States," I responded. "Kentucky." The blank stare remained until I said "Kentucky Fried Chicken" and his face brighten with understanding. We made awkward small talk for a while and then he invited me into his cousin's shop for tea.

Now joined by our tour guide, Chein, who spoke Vietnamese and English, I asked about his family. Nguyen had three children and two grandkids he noted. I bragged that I had three grandchildren. Asked if he had fought in the "American War," he nodded in the affirmative after Chein translated the question. Nguyen's facial expression never changed. He had served in the Southern and Western theaters from 1965-1975---and I thought my tour of duty of "365 days and a wake up" were bad! When pressed for more details I discovered that Nguyen had served near DaNang, South Vietnam at the same time I was flying combat missions in the F-4 Phantom and dodging rocket attacks at night.

I thought it ironic that while years earlier we might have exchanged gunfire, today we were exchanging stories about our grandchildren.

Nguyen emphasized with pride that he had served his country, defending his family and friends. I asked him what he feared the most as a soldier, hoping he'd point skyward and say he feared F-4 fighter pilots; but he straightened some and said he feared nothing. I was impressed. After a while we shook hands and went our separate ways.

What are the lessons I will take away from my two trips to Vietnam, first as a warrior and then as a missionary? On the rational, intellectual level I'm at peace with my experience. I believe my country made a mistake in getting involved in Southeast Asia though I think, for the most part, our intentions were good based on what we knew at the time. Would I go and fight again? Yes, based on what I understood at the time, I believed my participation was honorable. I was doing my duty for my country that I have sworn to defend against all enemies foreign and domestic.

On an emotional level I am at peace, too. Though I never experienced an intense, obvious emotional response following my mission trip, the lingering questions were confronted. I am at peace with my past now because I have been to Vietnam and for the first time I have come to know the Vietnamese people, even if only superficially. I have come to respect them for their work ethic and their love of country. After 10 years fighting the Americans, Nguyen could forgive America and it soldiers.

Still I struggled wanting to grab hold of that profound truth that lay beneath the surface. I wanted to have a great insight. I wanted to be able to say "Yes, finally, I've got it." The great revelation never came in terms I expected. The greatest truths are often the simplest. Jesus said: "Love your enemies. Do good to those who despitefully use you." God loves the Vietnamese people. He loves my former enemy, and I must also.

Barney Fife goes to the weight room.

My recent bouts with gout crippled my exercise program. A runner for over 30 years, I was inactive for over a month with inflamed, swollen and painful joints in my feet. I formulated a plan to gradually get back into shape and made my way to the Southeast Activities Center. We are fortunate to have such a splendid facility with the latest equipment and a professional staff to help you get your physical body in shape Monday through Friday, just as you get a spiritual workout with worship on the weekend and Bible study at other times.

I started by jogging easily for a mile. Normally I run for 30 minutes so I decided to supplement my brief run by riding a stationary bicycle for another 20 minutes. The bike has a gauge that measures your heart rate, and I watched my heart rate climb slowly from 60 to 125. I dismounted with my thighs pounding and my legs a little wobbly, unaccustomed to the biking exercise.

On my way out, I paused to checkout a large, brightly colored wall chart that depicted the amount of aerobic exercise gained from various levels of exertion. The chart plotted age versus heart rate needed to get aerobic conditioning. I found my age toward the far right edge, barely visible on the margin of the chart. I traced my age up to see what heart rate was necessary to achieve the requisite amount of exercise and wouldn't have been surprised to read a footnote which said: "At your age if you have a heartbeat, that's good enough." That was comforting, I thought to myself, and I limped toward the weight room resolving to restore my upper body back into shape overnight.

I didn't anticipate any problems since I have lifted weights in the past. At 5'5 ½" and 135 pounds, I needed to lift weights to bulk up for high school football. Later, while flying supersonic jets, I spent time in the weight room to increase my "g" tolerance. Adding muscle in the lower torso and legs helps a pilot resist blacking out during air-to-air combat, and it's always a good thing when a pilot of a single seat aircraft remains conscious throughout most of the flight.

I tried to look confident when I sauntered into the weight room after my exercise hiatus. I began pumping iron confident that in a few days *Body Building Magazine* would be clamoring for my picture to appear on their front cover. I wanted to wear one of those big belts like the real lifters wear, but couldn't find one so I just took the belt off my pants and cinched it up real tight. I'm sure I looked more like Barney Fife than Hulk Hogan when I asked to use the machine that would firm up my "abs" and strengthen my "pecks."

You know how those weight rooms walls are covered with mirrors so the lifters can admire their carefully sculpted bodies? Somebody apparently played a cruel joke on me and substituted one of those distorted mirrors you see at the circus, the kind that makes you look grotesquely short and fat. I complained to our Sports and Fitness Minister about the distortion in the mirror but he was unsympathetic. "Waddell," he said, "You *are* short and fat."

I had paid careful attention during my weight room orientation but that was many years ago, and it was so complicated I couldn't keep up. The instructor advised me to read the instructions on the machine if I needed to. Having to read instructions while lifting weights is a new concept for me. It used to be so simple when I was in high school. The instructions then were: 1. Lift barbell over your head. 2. Put it back down again.

I sat down at my first machine and stared at the instructions on the Cybex Dual Axis Incline Press through my "granny" glasses. I remembered that in high school I could press about a bezillion pounds so taking into account my age, I prudently set the machine for a half of a bezillion and pressed mightily against the bar grunting like those behemoths at the Olympics. It didn't move. I mean it didn't even budge. I was crestfallen.

I moved to the next machine recently vacated by a young lady in her mid-twenties. Having learned my lesson from the previous attempt to lift half a bezillion pounds I opted to swallow my pride and just use the weight the young lady was using anticipating that the bar would go flying heavenward. It didn't move either.

I moved to the curl machine to work on my biceps. Sitting on the other curl machine next to me was a "bemuscled" gentleman who looked a lot like he'd just come off the set of Baywatch. I thought it only fair to warn him that I'd be setting the machine at 37.5 pounds and I didn't want to make him look bad. He asked: "Haven't I seen you on Mayberry RFD reruns?"

I strained to finish my workout and considering my month long layoff probably overdid it just a bit...well, maybe a lot. That evening Nancy cut my meat for me and helped me lift my fork to my mouth. As always she was sympathetic to my moaning and groaning. "That's not the stupidest thing you've ever done," she opined, "but it's close."

As I considered my recent experience, it occurred to me that while my upper body strength was pretty good at one time, I had let the muscles atrophy by not exercising them regularly. It also occurred to me that I need to participate in daily spiritual exercise to prevent my spiritual body from becoming weak and vulnerable. A daily workout of prayer, devotions, quiet time and Bible reading is absolutely essential to keep my spiritual body in good shape. Physical exercise can increase the quality and length of your life on earth. Spiritual exercise can have the same effect on you spiritually.

"For physical training is of some value, but godliness has value for all things, holding promise for both the present life and the life to come."
1 Timothy 4:8

2,678 sermons without a fatality

It's always unnerving when you hear your name used in a sermon. In 2004, our senior minister, Bob Russell was talking about the courage of Moses in stepping out of his comfort zone to lead the Jews out of Egypt and into the Promised Land. Bob then said that in a similar way, I had accepted new responsibilities at Southeast by becoming the point of contact for some social and cultural issues. I must confess it was startling to hear my name, but it was also flattering to be mentioned from the pulpit in the same sentence as one of the Old Testament patriarchs.

At the time, my parents were vacationing in Florida so I called them Sunday evening knowing they'd want to share in my good fortune. When my mother answered the phone I said, "I just wanted to let you know that your son was used as an illustration in the sermon today." I guessed she sensed my need to be humbled, so she responded, "Which son?" I was crushed. "Mom!!" I protested. Unmoved, my mother then asked, "Was it a good illustration or a bad one."

Very few of the numerous sermons I have ever listened to have used me as either a good or a bad illustration even though I have listened to a lot of sermons. I'm pretty sure I've listened to 2,678 sermons in my life. If you want to check my math here's how it goes. (Remember I was an English major in college.) I started "listening" to sermons when I was seven. In those days we didn't have elaborate programs for the kids as we do now. In those days, you sat with your parents on hard pews (not plush theater seats) and listened to the sermon whether you wanted to or not. (We also walked 5 miles to school in the snow.)

At the time I figured this out I was 58 ½. So 58 ½ years minus 7 years old times 52 Sundays a year equals 2,678 sermons. Granted in the past 51.5 years I have missed a Sunday or two so the total might be lower except you must remember that Sundays in our church used to include two sermons, one in the morning and one in the evening. I never understood the double dose back then. Perhaps we were more sinful, I don't know.

Anyway, whatever the actual total of sermons, I've listened to a lot of them and I consider myself something of a sermon expert. I've heard some good ones and some bad ones (but not at Southeast!) and some in between. The longest sermon I endured was over an hour. Having grown up on a steady sermon diet of 30 minutes duration and three main points, I found that I became very uncomfortable as the preacher spoke on and on and on. After half an hour, my mind was more on my bladder than my Bible. I was reminded of Mark Twain's observation. "Few sinners are saved after the first twenty minutes of a sermon."

Actually I've discovered that there is a Biblical precedent for long sermons. The sermon Paul delivered to the Troas congregation during his third missionary journey was longer than 30 minutes. Acts 20 records that he "kept on talking until midnight...Seated in a window was a young man named Eutychus, who was sinking into a deep sleep as Paul talked on and on."

As Luke records the incident, Eutychus dozed off and fell to his death. For many it was probably just the interruption they needed and some headed off to tend to poor Eutychus (whose name ironically means "fortunate" in Greek) while others made a beeline for the first century equivalent of the restroom. Eutychus was miraculously healed by Paul and both returned to the third floor where Paul kept on preaching until daylight. You had to admire Paul's stamina, if not his brevity, since he was leaving for Assos the first thing in the morning.

In preparing to teach a class on Paul's fatal sermon, I discovered that there have been other fatal speeches in our history. After his election as our ninth president, William Henry Harrison prepared his inaugural address, which was delivered on a cold, rainy day in Washington on March 4, 1841. He insisted on delivering his address without a hat or overcoat and spoke for two hours. President Harrison contracted pneumonia and died a month later.

A friend shared with me a similar story about Alben Barkley, one of Kentucky's greatest politicians. On April 30, 1956 Barkley traveled to Lexington, Virginia to give a keynote speech to students of Washington and Lee University. There he quoted from Psalm 84:10 that he "would rather be a servant in the house of the lord than to sit in the seat of the mighty." At the conclusion of the address, he suffered a fatal heart attack. When I was Southeast's Director of Facilities that was my favorite Scripture, but I don't quote it anymore.

After listening to 2,678 sermons (none of which involved a fatality) I have come to realize one important point. There are no long or short, good or bad sermons. Every time a minister opens his mouth and shares the Gospel with us, God speaks to us clearly if we listen with an expectant and uncritical spirit, and if we focus on the message and not the messenger. I like the way Charles Finney put it: "Great sermons lead the people to praise the preacher. Good preaching leads the people to praise the Savior."

We are so fortunate at Southeast to be regaled weekly with sermons that are Bible-based, convicting and engaging. Each time Bob, Dave or Kyle step into the pulpit we are blessed by an insightful, scriptural message that is delivered with wisdom, humor and grace. These are truly sermons that allow us to praise the preacher <u>and</u> the Savior.

My annual trip to pediatric "purgatory"

Once a year, on Easter Weekend, I volunteer to work in the nursery. This is not an activity I would do under normal circumstances. Actually, I would rather fly combat than work in the nursery. While I love kids, working with them is definitely not my gift and certainly not my passion. I just don't have the patience for it. Who wants to spend an hour or so, surrounded by a dozen infants crying for no good reason, soiling their diapers unnecessarily and basically making my life miserable?

However, I volunteer to work in the nursery for three reasons:

1. The need is great, especially during Easter, and I want to do my part to help.

2. Working in the nursery is my annual penitence for past sins. I call it "pediatric purgatory." I'm sure this is not a theologically correct term from a Protestant perspective but you get my point.

3. More to the point, in my position as Involvement Minister, it is my job to encourage people to volunteer and serve in many areas of ministry, so I guess I should volunteer, too.

Anyway, I reported for duty in the nursery welcome center at 8:15 a.m. where a dozen or so other sleepy-eyed volunteers and I received an orientation briefing from Linda Brandon, Director of Early Children's Ministry. Linda is extremely well organized, and "runs a tight ship." (That's high praise from my Naval counterparts.) She delivered her briefing in such a professional and business-like manner I had flashbacks to basic training and my drill instructor. It was clear this was serious business, and we were going to do our job well. I instinctively responded, "Sir, yes sir...I mean ma'am" when the briefing was completed.

I learned that I was going to be what is known as a "floater." The title doesn't suggest a very prestigious position, but one I could master with some coaching, Linda offered optimistically. I was further advised that when I reported to my duty location, I was to don a blue or green smock and follow the instructions of the individual wearing the red smock who was the person in charge. I can still remember being a Colonel, i.e. the person in charge, so when I later entered the nursery room, I was tempted to grab one of the red smocks. I feared a mutiny of two year olds might ensue if I assumed the mantle of leadership, so I humbly put on a blue smock. Blue's my favorite color anyway, I rationalized.

Sergeant, I mean, Linda Brandon handed me my assignment with a wry smile. "Oh, Don," Linda announced "you go to nursery room E-3" as if my lofty position on the church staff had earned me a select group of kids. It was a select group all right. She gave me directions on how to get to E-3. "Left, left, right" she said. For those of us with military backgrounds this sounded for all the world like marching instructions so I skipped down the hall (left, left, right) feeling a little silly, but not nearly as silly as I was going to look with my blue or green smock.

I was sweating profusely as I entered E-3, due more to my apprehension than the exercise of skipping. I was one of the first to arrive. As you probably know, in many states there is a mandatory ratio of children to adult workers, something like one adult for every four to six kids, or some such. In my opinion the law is far too generous, and we exceeded my personal ratio when the first kid arrived.

After I got over my uneasiness and apprehension, I truly enjoyed the experience. All the kids were great. There was Aileen, Joy, Robert, Aubrey, Shelby, John, and Laura. They were as cute as they could be. Aileen sat on my lap as I read about David and Goliath and stuck by my side the entire time. I was flattered.

Our teacher, Julie, was awesome. I marveled at her organization. She was so enthusiastic and employed a variety of techniques to keep the kids' attention while she shared some spiritual truths with them. (She taught me some techniques I may be able to apply to the adult Sunday School class I teach. I think in the future we may include more cutting and pasting, for instance.) I assisted Julie by writing the child's name on glitter-covered crosses the kids prepared. I never saw so much glitter in all my life and when I showered the next day I rinsed a handful or so out of my hair.

What did I learn from my experience in the nursery? First, our children's department is extremely well organized and capably administered. Parents can feel confident that their children will be safe and spiritually fed. I came to more fully appreciate the job our staff does and especially the selfless efforts of thousands of volunteers who regularly work in the children's department. My once a year trek to the nursery is nothing compared to the sacrificial efforts of our regular volunteers.

Second, my experience reminded me how important our children are and how vital they are to the future of the Christ's church. Billy Graham has said that "Christianity is one generation away from extinction." This observation highlights the importance of passing on our spiritual beliefs and heritage to our children. It is vitally important that we inculcate our beliefs at an early age to give our children a sound foundation to carry them through life. Someone said, "Give me a child till he is 7 and I care not who gets him after that." This early training in the formative years of a child's development is absolutely essential. Proverbs 22:6 puts it this way: "Train a child in the way he should go, and when he is old he will not turn from it."

Finally, I was reminded how important these kids are to Jesus. In Mark 10 Jesus said, "Let the little children come to me, and do not hinder them, for the kingdom of God belongs to such as these. I tell you the truth, anyone who will not receive the kingdom of God like a little child will never enter it." Maybe I got a glimpse of what Heaven will be like when I worked in the nursery on Easter. All in all, it was a rewarding experience and I'll probably volunteer for nursery duty again...in about 365 days.

Men being men; it's a scary thing to watch

The smell of testosterone was in the air as my two sons, Don the 4th and David, and their cousin, Charlie and I loaded the fishing tackle into Don's boat. You could cut the male bonding with a knife as the four of us made our pre-dawn departure for the high seas. Conditions were perfect for a real manly event, in a word they were miserable.

During our recent vacation to Panama City, Florida the weather had been terrible but by Friday the sea state had calmed to 2-4 feet and the guys seized the opportunity to get away for some deep-sea fishing. We all knew it would be rough, but we were men and we were going to accomplish this adventure "come hell or high water" and on this day it looked like both were a distinct possibility.

Don had some problems starting the engine and then the rain increased in intensity. Every man on board wondered if we should really go, but no one dared ask the question. That would be, well, unmanly, so the question was never asked.

Finally the engine started, and we made our way out of the bay into the gulf. I remembered then why I had joined the Air Force instead of the Navy. (Winston Churchill described going to sea like going to prison with the opportunity to drown.) The 2-4 foot waves may not sound too bad but were high enough that the boat was almost completely out of the water much of the time, and then we came slamming down repeatedly with an enormous, tooth-rattling crash.

I had recurring visions of "A Perfect Storm" in my mind and eventually my son started to bare a noticeable resemblance to George Clooney. The rain was only a minor irritant compared to dodging thunderstorms and waterspouts. "We better head west," counseled Charlie, who had more experience sailing than the rest of us. After dodging several small storms I think I saw Galveston, Texas in the distance and suggested east might be an appropriate option.

The waves calmed a bit as we made our way into the open sea. I was on the bow assuming my most resolute Captain Ahab pose. My face was set to the wind, the sea spray covering my face. I had my ball cap turned backward on my head. My sunglasses were obscured by rain. "This is great," I yelled to my fellow adventurers but deep down inside I was miserable. It was about this time that David became sea sick. He claimed he was just chumming for fish, but we knew better and teased him unmercifully as he shared his breakfast with the fish.

Don had planned for the trip meticulously. We had studied the weather reports on the Weather Channel. I had logged on to the Internet and gotten real time sea state measurements from a buoy located near our intended fishing spot. Don had acquired geodetic survey maps showing the location of sunken ships, which might attract a large number of fish. We navigated to the fishing hole with the aid of satellites beaming down Global Positioning System information. Finally when we got to the general area, Don used his sonar fish finder to put us right over the spot where the fish were. All this high tech equipment was used to outwit a school of fish with a collective IQ of minus two. Go figure.

But outsmart those pesky Pisces we did, reeling in several respectable groupers and red snappers. As I stared down at our catch for the day and considered the cost of all the equipment required for the expedition, I figured the fish cost about $513 per pound. That was an insignificant consideration, however. They would taste all the better for dinner that night. Today we were the 21st Century equivalent of our primordial ancestors. We were the hunter-gathers for our family. No, there would be no hunger at the Waddell household today. We had prevailed. We had conquered the elements. We were men.

This tale is only slightly exaggerated, Walter Mitty style, to make a point. That is that there is within every man a desire for adventure, a need for conquest. In his best-selling book, *Wild At Heart*, John Eldredge claims that unfortunately our culture, especially our churches have made men into "nice boys" who are too cautious and careful to achieve their God-given potential.

Writes Eldredge: "Too many men forsake their dreams because they aren't willing to risk, or fear they aren't up to the challenge, or are never told that those desires deep in their heart are good. But the soul of a man, the real gold... isn't made for controlling things; he's made for adventure." He continues: "A man's life becomes an adventure, [and the] whole thing takes on a transcendent purpose when he releases control in exchange for the recovery of the dreams in his heart."

Of course, the ultimate adventure isn't deep-sea fishing, hunting in Alaska or racing down the hill on a Colorado ski slope. Having flown fighter aircraft in combat I would also suggest that the ultimate adventure isn't even flying combat. The ultimate adventure is when you risk it all and turn your life completely over to God and say "lead me where You will."

God has a plan for all of us regardless of gender. And many of the plans will never be realized unless we are willing to risk it all, throw caution to the wind and be a "fool for Christ," to paraphrase the Apostle Paul's words. I think my life has been pretty adventurous flying combat and supersonic fighters.

But the biggest risk I took in my life was forsaking our Florida retirement plans, selling our retirement home in Fort Walton Beach and returning to Louisville so I could work in my home church and thus begin the most rewarding and thrilling adventure of my life as a minister at Southeast.

How much adventure do you have in your life? Would you risk it all if you knew there were greater rewards to be had? God may be calling you, as he called Abraham, Moses, Paul, and others to trust Him and live a life beyond the mundane, to be "wild at heart."

57 is a good age if you're a steak sauce

How do you feel about birthdays? My secretary, Kristen Evans loves them, but she's young and gregarious. For my part, I hate birthdays. My idea of a really happy birthday is me singing "Happy Birthday To Me" in the shower before I go to work and everyone else ignoring my "special day." Unfortunately, that seldom happens, and this particular year was no exception.

I was 57 on June 7, 2002. Now 57 is a good age if you're a Sequoia in a national forest in California. 57 is a great number if you're steak sauce. 57 is a good age if you a contemporary of Methuselah or someone else who is 900+ years old. But 57, for me, is the pits and birthday celebrations are only a painful reminder of how old I really am.

It's an awkward age too since at 57, you reap few of the benefits of being old. Sure you are eligible to subscribe to AARP, but that privilege, it seems, now comes shortly after birth. Senior discounts don't usually kick in till later, and there's no social security checks showing up in the mail. Meanwhile your body is showing the effects of almost six decades of wear and tear.

The hair on top of your head has moved to your nostrils and ears. Ugly red spots appear in other areas. Buttons are more difficult to fasten. Skin ointments and lotions you used to see only in your grandmother's medicine cabinet now populate your bathroom. Getting out of bed in the morning takes longer and is accompanied by creeks and groans. We middle aged people are constantly reminded of our nearing obsolescence, so why do people go out of their way to celebrate this unfortunate circumstance?

This year was the worst as far a birthday parties were concerned. There was one event after another recognizing the fact that I am now "over the hill," or "older than dirt." First there was a dinner party two days before my birthday with my parents and my nephew, Mike. Mike, was born on my birthday so it's one of the few I don't forget.

Then on June 7th, the 57th anniversary of a very painful experience for Doris Waddell, my office was decorated with balloons and sarcastic signs making fun of the geriatric population, which presumably includes me.

Then my coworkers took me out to lunch amid much merriment, good cheer and old jokes. There were more cards and presents and wrapping paper.

Then as if my fun meter wasn't already pegged, my birthday this year coincided with the first annual Cornerstone ABF retreat. (ABF stands for Adult Bible Fellowship, or Sunday School by another name.) I hoped they might overlook the birthday. No such luck. There was more cake and ice cream, more gifts, more abuse.

As I reflected on the agony of enduring multiple reminders of how old I am, I decided that there are at least four reasons I don't like birthdays.

1. They are an inescapable reminder of how old you are. I assume everyone who says "happy birthday" is well intended, but to me they are just rubbing salt in the wounds. People look at you as if they were talking to a tree or the

mummified remains of King Tut and then say: "You're only 57 years old. You don't look *that* old." How do you respond to that statement? "I'm glad I look great even though I have one foot in the grave."

2. Birthdays are an inescapable reminder of what a clod I am. Every June 7th my good buddy and high school friend, Sandy Robertson calls me at work and sings "Happy Birthday" to me. She is sweet and thoughtful, but her birthday greeting only serves to remind me, annually, that I forgot her birthday the day before.

3. Birthdays are fattening. The older you get, the harder it is to keep the pounds off and all the cake and ice cream doesn't help. It's not too harmful for the participants but for the aging guest of honor, who has to attend multiple birthday parties, the calories add up pretty quickly. I mean, we're not taking about tofu and bean sprouts. There are some serious calories here.

4. People who won't normally even say "hello" are compelled to say nice things to you or worse yet, hug you as if it might be their last opportunity to interact with you before you die. You also get cards from people you only hear from once a year, such as your realtor, insurance agent, or investment counselor. This year I got a card from the group who gave me a hearing test ten months ago. I was moved beyond words or maybe I just didn't hear the words I said.

I've heard it observed that growing old is the pits, but it sure beats the alternative, and I must admit that I have been truly blessed to have lived this long. If I had lived at the turn of the 20th Century, I would have died 7 years ago since the average life span then was only 50.

God has been so good to me and, when viewed in that context, birthdays are an annual reminder of God's goodness and the fact that I am actually nearer to spending eternity with Him. With that in mind, I wonder if we'll have birthday parties in heaven? I hope not. Perhaps we'll have parties recognizing our spiritual birthday, the day we were born again by accepting Christ and being baptized.

In John 3:3-5 Jesus told Nicodemus about his spiritual birthday when he said, 'I tell you the truth, no one can see the kingdom of God unless he is born again.' 'How can a man be born when he is old?' Nicodemus asked. 'Surely he cannot enter a second time into his mother's womb to be born!' Jesus answered, 'I tell you the truth, no one can enter the kingdom of God unless he is born of water and the Spirit.'

If you're playing golf after you die, you're not in heaven.

You may have heard about the two Christians who loved to play golf. During one of their rounds they speculated as to whether or not there would be golf in Heaven, and they resolved that whoever died first would find a way to contact the partner who was still alive and tell them whether or not there was golf in Heaven. Not long afterwards, one of the golfers did die and appeared to his friend in a dream. "Hank," said the one in Heaven, "I've got great news, there is golf in heaven! Unfortunately, the bad news is that we have a tee time this Friday."

I have been a golfer for ten years and after a decade of frustration, slices, shanks, and duck hooks, I cannot imagine why God would allow such a bedeviling game to be played in Paradise. Yet, I must confess that the game has consumed me since I started playing in 1990. Prior to this time, I played occasionally, but being a parent didn't allow me much time for golf. However, at age 45 my kids were essentially on their own, and I went to work for a two-star general who was an avid golfer. General Chambers said: "Waddell, you need to learn to play golf. You'll never get promoted to general officer if you can't play golf."

Being a dutiful subordinate who wanted to get promoted, I saluted smartly and went to our local golf course and bought a set of golf clubs. I never did get promoted to General, but I did get stuck with a game that won't let go of me. I am not proud of the fact that I spent countless hours at the practice range over the years trying to hit a stupid ball ten yards farther. I'm a little ashamed that I spent many dollars on lessons. I occasionally regret that I spent a portion of my children's inheritance on high tech golf equipment.

To probe deeper into the question about golf in Heaven, I took an informal survey of the church staff and our Thursday morning golf league and 76% said "yes, there is golf in heaven." Dave Stone dissented citing Revelation 21: "There will be no more sorrow, nor crying, neither shall there be any more pain."

There are a lot of reasons why there will be no golf in heaven. There won't be golf in heaven because my wife said so. She's never really approved of my obsession with golf. She can nag me all she wants about golfing in heaven but I've got news for her…there's not going to be any marriage in heaven either.

I searched diligently but there is no mention of "golf' in the Bible. Closest I could come was 2 Tim 4:7 where Paul said he had "finished my course."

Additionally, while there's lots of grace in Heaven, there is no grace in golf. Read the rule book. No gimme putts, improving your lie, or mulligans. But there is lots of grace in heaven. Can you imagine stepping up to the number one tee box in Heaven, teeing the ball up and God says: "The rest of that is good. Pick it up." That won't work.

Golf is a four-letter word and they'll be no swearing in heaven. Why is it called "golf"? All the other four-letter words were taken according to Dr. Vincent Manjoney. Playing with some of my secular friends is a spiritual activity. They are always referring to God, until they remember I'm a minister.

Don't think that's what Paul had in mind when he told us to pray without ceasing. "If profanity had an influence on the flight of the ball, the game would be played far better that it is," according to Horace Hutchison

I'm so glad General Chambers ordered me to take up the game, because as a result I have come to know and love my golfing buddies. If it weren't for golf I might never have known many really swell, God-loving guys, and I would have missed the special relationships that are part of the Southeast Men's Golf League.

In the final analysis, the thing that has kept me playing golf has nothing to do with 250 yard drives, a 15' putt for an eagle or a round in the 70s. I have kept playing golf because I like golfers. Senior PGA golfer George Archer said it this way: "Golf is like fishing and hunting. What counts is the companionship and fellowship of friends, not what you catch or shoot."

In writing to Philemon Paul put it this way: Philemon 1:4-7 "I always thank my God as I remember you in my prayers, because I hear about your faith in the Lord Jesus and your love for all the saints. I pray that you may be active in sharing your faith, so that you will have a full understanding of every good thing we have in Christ. Your love has given me great joy and encouragement, because you, brother, have refreshed the hearts of the saints."

I really felt that special relationship during one round in 2005 in particular. It was a beautiful Thursday morning, and some fog had settled in the low-lying areas. There was gentle breeze blowing. The sky was a deep blue and perfectly clear. It was the kind of splendid fall day that testified to the magnificence of our God and His creation.

At about 8:30, 32 men gathered in a circle in front of the clubhouse. Each man was very different individually, but we were all united in a commitment to our God and His son Jesus Christ. As we gathered together, we shared prayer requests and then we joined hands and prayed. And then I knew why I loved golf. I love golf because of golfers.

Ravi Zechariah, Christian philosopher and apologist who was born in India and educated at Cambridge, has said that a key to understanding the nature and character of God is found in relationships: Husband and wife, parent and child, among friends. In that circle of Christian brothers one Thursday morning, I felt the presence of God. And that's what Heaven is. Is there golf in heaven? The short answer is I don't know. But my golfing buddies have taught me that there's a little heaven in golf.

Caring for aging parents

Dave Stone preached a sermon many years ago on "Caring for Aging Parents." As always, Dave made some great points, and I sent a copy of the message to my kids as a reminder that my wife, Nancy and I might need some help in the future. They sent the sermon back to me.

The sermon also made me reflect on my relationship with my parents. My parents and I were asked to participate in a video featured as part of the sermon, and in the video I was supposed to tell what I was doing to care for my parents in their "old age." I wanted to say that since I have been designated as the executor of their estate, I felt like my primary job was to discourage any extravagant purchases that might diminish my inheritance. Just kidding.

The truth of the matter is that Don and Doris Waddell are about as independent and self-reliant as any people I know. (Dad has since died, but as of this writing mom is still very much alive and kicking.) Matter of fact, at the time of the interview it seems like they are helping me a lot more than I help them. Dad still paid for dinner when we ate out, and my parents have lent me money on several occasions. I value their advice and still seek their counsel often.

I am really proud of my parents, too. Both mom and dad have been active in the church and volunteered in a variety of activities. Dad has been counting the weekend offering for many years. Originally, he did this all by himself, and I can recall coming home to visit while stationed overseas. On Monday morning I'd come down for breakfast and the entire offering for SCC would be laid out on the kitchen table. I kid you not.

Dad was patiently counting the offering and entering contributions into the church records. "Dad" I scolded, "I don't think bringing the entire church offering to the house to be counted is a good idea." He appreciated my concern but dismissed my anxiety by noting that he took a different route to the bank each week. I'm not sure that would deter any "Bonnie and Clyde" wanna-be's but, in fact, he was never robbed at gunpoint on the way to the bank.

Mom was a stalwart in the adult library for many years and helped it grow from a handful of books to a professional program that rivals many secular libraries. While she is less active now than she used to be, she still participates in Women's Circles and visits shut-ins.

In the video I told how my parents modeled for me the process of caring for aging parents. My grandmother, Gladys White lived with us while I was growing up. As she aged, I watched my mom and dad devote more time to her. Their efforts were more than helping Gladys just get by as they provided love and dignity too, and included grandmother as an essential part of the family. Mom and dad keep her at home even when she was quite infirm and might have been put in a nursing home.

I have numerous examples of how involved my parents were in my life as I grew up. Mom was sometimes involved more than I expected or desired, if you know what I mean. Perhaps she was not as involved as the mother I saw on TV recently. I was channel surfing when I came upon a boxing match and was amazed to watch the mother of one boxer enter the ring and attack her son's opponent with her shoe. Now that's an involved mother.

The best story about my mom's involvement in my life occurred in 1959 and was a favorite story of the late Olin Hay, minister at South Louisville Christian Church where we attended while I was growing up. In 1959 I was halfback on Seneca's junior varsity football team. We were playing Atherton in Cherokee park. The makeshift field had no bleachers for spectators who crowded along the sidelines to see their classmate or child play.

Late in the second half, I was carrying the ball on a sweep toward the sideline where mom was leaning forward to see the play. She leaned so far forward that she not only saw, but became involved in the play. As Olin Hay told the story, she blocked three would-be tacklers and enabled me to run for a touchdown. While this story may have been embellished over the years, I distinctly remember looking back to see my mom on the ground amongst several other football players.

Dad didn't get physically involved in my activities, although I remember him being present at almost all my school activities despite the demands of his work. Dad's job didn't involve cross body blocks at a football game. Dad's job was rescuing me. I lost track of the number of times he came to help me late at night. In one case, I ran out of gas on I-65 perilously close to my curfew and delivering the gas after midnight involved a U turn across the interstate. Unfortunately a state trooper stopped dad for the illegal turn. As I recall, dad was not in the best of moods when he poured the gas into my car.

In another incident, I was returning from Boston, Kentucky early one cold, January Sunday morning when I had a flat tire. For reasons I can't recall I did not have the trunk key with me and had to call dad to be rescue me again. Unfortunately, during the return trip dad hit an icy curve in the road and slid into a ditch. Dad wasn't overly pleased as we waited for the tow truck to come and pull him out of the ditch.

All this is to say that I have been very blessed to have two loving Christian parents who helped me become a Christian parent myself. Years ago, they took care of me when I was unable to care for myself. Today, as Dave explained so well in his sermon, I have to be willing to do the same for them now, if required.

America is great because America good

In the spring of 1993 my wife and I drove to Berlin to attend the inactivation of an Air Force unit located at Templehof Air Base. The Iron Curtain had come down several years earlier, but East Germany was still laboring to recover from 43 years of Communism.

As we passed from what used to be West Germany into the former communist East, the difference was immediately apparent. Rusted barbed wire fences and abandoned guard towers at the border checkpoints were reminders of what amounted to a nation of people imprisoned by the Soviet Union and denied the basic freedoms most of us take for granted. The roads were noticeably rougher, the buildings were dirty and the people cheerless.

Nancy and I lamented the misfortune of the German people who had to endure subhuman conditions through the Nazi regime and four decades of Communist rule. What was the fundamental difference between the United States and the Soviet Bloc countries before the Iron Curtain crumbled? The difference was only words on a piece of paper. Pretty important words mind you, and a pretty important piece of paper.

When we observe Independence Day, it is appropriate to remind ourselves of the importance of this piece of paper, the Declaration of Independence. It was signed 217 years ago (at the time of this writing) and inaugurated the idea that this nation of people should live in freedom.

Obviously, July 4, 1776 was the seminal event in our nation's history. The Continental Congress adopted the Declaration of Independence in Philadelphia, and it was signed by 56 brave patriots, the vast majority of whom were orthodox Christians. Later the first Independence Day was celebrated in Philadelphia on July 8, 1776 with the reading of the document, ringing of bells and bands. Of course, we celebrate the holiday on the 4th of July, which only became a legal holiday in 1941.

The Declaration of Independence is a piece of paper without equal in the history of the world. Not only did it declare our independence from English rule, but it also set forth some basic rights of mankind. Our founding fathers wrote in part: "We hold these truths to be self-evident, that all men are created equal and endowed by their Creator with certain unalienable rights and that among these are life, liberty and the pursuit of happiness." These familiar and now immortal words laid the foundation for what has become the greatest democracy in history of civilization.

But this piece of paper isn't the only difference between the U.S. and other nations. The bigger difference is that this document acknowledged that there is a God and that our nation is established based on His divine providence. The French statesman, Alexis de Tocqueville studied the workings of democracy in the early part of the nineteenth century in order to understand America's success. Most of us are familiar with his concluding observation that: "America is great because America is good, and if America ever ceases to be good, America will cease to be great."

Fewer are familiar with the words that precede this conclusion. He said first, "I sought for the greatness and genius of America in her spacious harbors and her ample rivers, and it was not there. I sought for the greatness and genius of America in her rich mines and her vast world commerce, and it was not there. I sought for the greatness and genius of America in her public school system and her institutions of learning, and it was not there. I sought for the greatness and genius of America in her democratic congress and her matchless Constitution, and it was not there. Not until I went into the churches of America and heard her pulpits flame with righteousness did I understand the secret of her genius and power. America is great because America is good, and if America ever ceases to be good, America will cease to be great."

This should be a sobering reminder to Americans today. The headlines in our newspapers reveal that we are gradually surrendering our commitment to this fundamental truth that America is great because of God's blessing and not our own skill, resourcefulness and intelligence. It is time for us to rededicate ourselves to the basic Christian principles of our founding fathers, which includes trust in Almighty God. The Psalmist reminds us: "Blessed is the nation whose God is the Lord." Psalm 33:12. The writer of 2 Chronicles observed: "If My people who are called by my name, will humble themselves and pray and seek my face, and turn from their wicked ways then will I hear from heaven and will forgive their sin and will heal their land." 2 Chronicles 7:14

Unless we as a nation rededicate ourselves to the Christian beliefs upon which this nation was founded, until our pulpits again "flame with righteousness," we can expect continued social chaos and moral anarchy. We can expect to decline and die like superpowers of the past. As John Adams observed, "We have no government armed with power capable of contending with human passions unbridled by morality and religion...Our constitution was made only for a moral and religious people. It is wholly inadequate to the government of any other."

At least Job didn't have to worry about complete electrical failure

"Think of all the money we're saving on the electric bill," I said trying to console Nancy in the aftermath of the storm that left thousands without power. We were one of the thousands, but she was disconsolate. "What am I going to do without my hairdryer and curling iron?" she asked irritably.

Initially, the inconvenience was exciting, almost an adventure. I had Walter Middy-like fantasies and likened myself to our pioneer forefathers who contended with the elements without the benefit of all the modern conveniences. I imagined myself sitting by a roaring fire, reading by candlelight, hunting wild game for my family and coming home to my large screen TV and ESPN. It wasn't long before my 21st Century "adventure" became a real drag, but it seemed to affect each family member differently.

From my point of view, it wasn't that much of a problem... except for the smashed fingers. I got them attempting to close the garage door. Whoever designed the automatic doors didn't take into full consideration electrical failure. There was no handle for manual operation. The door was closing fine until my fingers got smashed as the interlocking panels came together. Ouch! There certainly was a lot of electricity in the air as I grabbed my fingers in pain.

I must confess the storm's aftermath affected me less than the other members of my family. You see, I got to go to work each day where the electricity worked fine. When I returned home however, I had to make some adjustments. Shaving by candlelight was a challenge. At the same time, television offered about the same entertainment value during complete electrical failure as it does with 150 amperes coursing through the wiring in our house. While I was at work I cooled off, recharged my cell phone and lap top batteries and returned home at the end of the day no worse for wear.

Nancy had to make more sacrifices---more than just her hair dryer and curling iron. She couldn't vacuum. This was a tragedy. Of course the iron and stove wouldn't know the difference between complete electrical failure and normal use. But no electricity also meant no air conditioning and heat is a real problem for people with MS, such as my wife. So she put her pillow under her arm, and we headed east, seeking refuge with my parents who had been spared the brunt of the storm. Actually Nancy can always use more quality time with her mother-in-law.

Mom and Nancy have a great relationship, but contending with Zac was another matter. He loves grandma's house where dropped morsels of food are more plentiful than at our house. He spends his entire time with his nose pressed to the floor looking for dropped crumbs. The sleeping arrangements, however, created a difficult situation. Zac normally sleeps in the utility room by himself...the salient words being "by himself." Nancy understandably tires of him in her lap or being underfoot constantly and she certainly doesn't want him in bed with her.

At grandma's house Zac slept upstairs in the bathroom next to us. But he loves his mom and couldn't contend with being just feet from her as she snored blissfully. He'd whimper, then sneeze (he always sneezes when he's serious) then yap, then he'd bark. I'd fuss at him and he'd be silent for a while. Needless to say, we didn't sleep very well that night and agreed he could spend the next night at home without electricity and air conditioning.

Now if you're a hyperactive, hypoallergenic Bichon Frise whose food comes packed in a can, complete electrical failure is a problem since the electric can opener doesn't work. I groped around in the kitchen with my flashlight the next morning wondering what to do. I vaguely remembered my grandmother opening cans with a mechanical device, but I hadn't even seen one in years.

Meanwhile, Zac paced the floor anxiously, occasionally bumping into furniture obscured by the darkness. I held the can in my hand and considered using a saw. Unfortunately, my only saw is an electric one. Hacking it open with a knife was a possibility. After rummaging around in the dark kitchen for a while I found a manual can opener and fed the dog. I was late to work that day, and I had developed a festering case of carpal tunnel syndrome in the process of opening the can.

As stressful as this was, it wasn't as bad as when we lost power during the storm in early June; that incident was considerably more challenging. We returned home from vacationing in Gatlinburg to find our house without a single watt of juice. That would have been bad enough but we had also brought back our eight and five year old grandsons. This was my worst nightmare: Two very active kids in my house and no TV, no video, no computer games. As the batteries began to run down on the kids' Game Boy I felt an immediate calling to a foreign mission field. Some remote location in deepest, darkest Africa began to look pretty good.

I suppose our individual reactions to this ordeal revealed something about our character. How do you respond to adversity? During the power outage I tried escapism, fleeing to work. Zac tried whining and barking. Nancy adapted to her new circumstances.

When faced with the storms of life or complete electrical failure all we can really do is trust God. It's the lesson of Job one more time.

Psalm 18:28 "You, Lord, keep my lamp burning; my God turns my darkness into light."

For poorer, for poorer

N ancy is fond of telling people that being married to me has provided her 25 years of marital bliss. Then she adds: "Unfortunately we've been married for 35 years."

On July 22nd 2002 we celebrated 35 years of marriage. I wanted to make it a special affair, so we booked a romantic river cruise on the Star of Louisville. Granted the Ohio River is not quite as romantic as the Seine or the Rhine where we have spent previous anniversaries, but considering our past it was OK. Our honeymoon in 1967 was unglamorous and cut short because I had to go to work on Monday.

But I wanted to make our 35th special and asked Nancy what I could buy her that would make her really happy. Actually, I was thinking of a new dress on sale at Walmart, a lifetime subscription to AARP, or membership at some ritzy golf country club. She said she really wanted an "Anniversary Ring." That sounded appropriate enough, but expensive.

Nancy and my daughter Dawn had done some looking around and found a "reasonable" ring for "about $700." I swallowed hard and forced a smile and said "we'll see." I did a quick cost benefit analysis in my head and noted that a $700 ring would equal about 25 rounds of golf, 239 Big Macs with fries, or half of that new laptop I desired. I mean I love her but... In vain, I reminded her of 1 Peter 3:3 "Your beauty should not come from outward adornment, such as braided hair and the wearing of gold jewelry and fine clothes."

So we trundled off to the jewelers on one sunny Saturday morning when most self-respecting men were on the golf course or getting pumped up for the Atlanta Braves baseball game that afternoon. I had an uneasy feeling when I learned that Nancy had talked to my mother in between her preliminary search for an anniversary ring and our outing. Mom recommended a jewelry store closer to us and "nicer." Noticeably absent in her description of the jewelry store were the words "cheap, reasonable, or you won't have to work another 35 years to pay for it."

I knew I was in trouble when we entered the store and the sales lady met us at the door with a smile. She escorted us to an overstuffed chair next to the display counter and asked what we wanted to drink. This is not Walmart, I thought as I glanced at my watch. There was only 45 minutes until the Braves game and this was obviously going to take longer than I had planned.

The sales lady, Ruth, swept her hand gracefully over the panoply of sparkling gems and asked what "we" wanted to see. The first person plural pronoun was not exactly accurate since only one of us really wanting to buy something. When Nancy said she wanted an anniversary ring, the lady began to visibly salivate and directed our attention to a display case with stones about the size of the baseball about to be thrown out in Atlanta. I began to sweat profusely as I noticed the price tags on the two and three carat gems. The smallest diamond was 1/10 of a carat. "Do you have something less than a 1/10 of a carat?" I asked earnestly. Ruth looked at me like I had just asked if she wanted to buy some of my Enron or WorldCom stock, two companies being investigated at the time by the Attorney General.

To her credit, Nancy noted that she had a petite hand and was looking for a smaller anniversary ring pointing to a grouping in the $500 section. My attitude took a decide turn to the positive while a look of shock swept over Ruth's face. "Oh, no. That's not for you," Ruth said quickly, "Those diamonds are of inferior quality." "Our friends won't be able to tell," I retorted, "I almost never see any of them wearing a jeweler's magnifying glass at church."

Nancy tried on several rings each a little larger than the previous one. "Remember your petite hand," I kept saying. (This decision was taking far too long. It looked now like my only hope to see the ballgame was if it went into extra innings.) Finally she settled on a ring with not one, not a half dozen, but 14 diamonds. "Excellent choice," Ruth said shielding the price tag from my sight. "That's 1.03 carats."

I did some quick math in my head. The 1/3 carat cost $700, then the one carat must be...yowee! That's more than we paid for our first car when we were married 35 years ago. Ruth acknowledged the cost but comforted us with the reminder that the ring came with a lifetime warranty. "Big deal," I thought "at our age we don't even buy green bananas."

So we bought the ring and I am back in the running for "Husband of the Year." I told Nancy she had to tell the kids she had spent their entire inheritance on a ring. They'll have to fight over it when we die. I wish I could be around to see that!

As we left the store, I had to support Nancy's hand because of the weight of the ring, and now I have to wear sunglasses in her presence. Meanwhile, Ruth was already on the phone calling her investment counselor making plans for an early retirement.

But the ring is pretty and it's a nice reminder of the 35 wonderful years it represents. But we can't take credit for this accomplishment. God brought Nancy and I together at a church hayride on a blind date in July 1961. The intervening years have been wonderful (maybe even more than the 25 years of bliss Nancy claims!) because God has blessed us as we committed our lives and family to Him on July 22, 1967 when we each promised "to have and to hold, from this day forward; for better, for worse, for richer, for poorer; in sickness and in health, to love and to cherish till death do us part..." Somehow the "for poorer" part seems more appropriate now after our trip to the jewelers.

To increase the romance, stay out of the hot tub

Recently a friend recommended that I take Nancy on an extended romantic getaway, just the two of us, no grandkids, no cellphone, no laptop. (My hands started to shake uncontrollably. I could almost see a romantic getaway without Nancy, but without my cellphone and laptop??) Anyway, my wise friend recognized that the stress and strain of ministry can take a toll on couples and wisely encouraged us to go on an extended vacation.

The military has a similar program called "R&R," or rest and relaxation. I benefited from it many times, twice while serving in a combat zone. (Now I am not trying to equate marriage and combat, but there are parallels in some relationships.) R&R recognizes the necessity of allowing the troops to have a time to recover from intense operations so they can continue to perform at a high level.

So, following the advice of our friend, Nancy and I recently booked ourselves on an Alaskan cruise this summer as part of our 45th wedding anniversary.

I almost immediately had flashbacks to our 37th anniversary when Nancy and I took a brief getaway to a beautiful house overlooking the Ohio that the church owned and rented out to the staff for R&R. I remember our first evening there. We considered where to go for our anniversary dinner. We've celebrated previous anniversaries with dinners in Paris (France, not Kentucky), Bavaria, the Orient and other romantic places. This time we went to a Mexican restaurant in Prospect, Kentucky. When you answer the call of God to go into all the world, sometimes you end up in Prospect.

We returned home to watch a mindless video and wandered off to bed at 10:00. Nancy donned her "Born to Sleep" PJs, and I was asleep before my head hit the pillow. When we were 22 and newly married this is not the way we would have anticipated our 37th anniversary ending, but in 2004 it was just fine...so much for romance. It's still there; it's just different.

In addition to rest, we were also looking for relaxation, but I have discovered that there is a fine line between relaxation and boredom. Often I can't tell the difference.

For me relaxation began in earnest on day two of our romantic getaway. I slept like a lamb until 5:30 a.m., about 30 minutes longer than normal. I have learned over the years that the most thoughtful, considerate thing I can do for my bride is let her sleep in the morning. So I tiptoed out of the room, fixed a pot of coffee and proceeded to do my devotions in an unhurried manner.

As peaceful as my morning devotions were, however, the next hour was anything but. What I am going to share with you now was not my fault. There were no instructions on how to operate the hot tub, a novelty I had never used before. I have nothing against hot tubs, but you have to invest a lot of time to get the full benefit of a hot tubs and to be honest I have better things to do with my time than sit around in large tub of hot water and let jets of water massage my body while my skin shrivels up to resemble an albino raisin.

Had there been instructions for the hot tub, I'm sure they would have said: "Do not turn water pumps on until the tub is completely full." I did not know about this operational procedure, so you can imagine my surprise when I hit the "on" switch and rather than hot, churning, bubbling water, I got two streams of water arching across the bathroom toward the toilet 15 feet away. (It was a very large bathroom.)

If there had been a three-alarm fire in the commode, it would have been extinguished in a matter of seconds. I have never seen so much water on the floor in all my life. Actually, mopping up a bathroom floor was not part of my agenda for my relaxing time away.

Despite the misadventures, we enjoyed being alone together. It was just the two of us removed from the crush of our often hectic routine, enjoying not only each other but our relationship.

But there was a spiritual component to our getaway as well. I had a wonderful time with God during my morning devotions, sitting on the porch overlooking the Ohio as the sun rose in the east. It was a profoundly spiritual experience. I sat there for an hour reading my Bible and praying. In that setting it was easier to praise God, the creator of the universe. I had no schedule, no "to do" list, nothing to rush out and do. There was little to distract me or compete for my time with God. It was a time to "be still and know" that He is God. I thought of David who wrote in Psalm 5:3 "In the morning, O LORD, you hear my voice; in the morning I lay my requests before you and wait in expectation."

Now, we are looking forward expectantly to a relaxing time together on our cruise in July, however Nancy has ordered that I stay away from the hot tub unless I have adult supervision.

Our hyperactive, hypoallergenic, hyper allergenic, hypochondriac dog

I've been working at the church for seven years now. It's been a great time full of fantastic experiences and encounters with wonderful people each with an uplifting story of how their lives have been changed. Still, when I run into friends in the atrium they usually don't ask about how many new members we've involved in ministries. They don't ask how many people I've led to Christ. No, the question I am asked the most is: "How's Zac?"

Zac is our five-year old Bichon Frise puppy. He has come into our family and taught us much about life and given us a spiritual insight or two as well. One thing he has taught us is that another child would have been cheaper than a dog. I read recently that the lifetime cost of a dog is about $6400. I'm pretty sure we've paid at least that much in medical bills alone the first year. I mean it's been one thing after another.

Zac's afflicted with allergies. We tried pills, shots and steroids, but the scratching continued. I could handle the pet antihistamines, pills and shots. I could even deal with the steroids, which made him fairly assertive and perpetually hungry. We often found him barking at his bowl, as if he could create some puppy chow with the sound of his voice. But I drew the line at bringing in a pet allergist for advice. The dog can scratch for all I care. Isn't that what dogs do?

Finally the vet put Zac on a special diet to treat his allergies. Are you ready for this? Zac was put on a strict diet of duck and potato. La De Da. The first time I fed him his new diet I put a napkin over my wrist. We dispensed with candlelight and strolling strings, but I considered serving the La Duck with a hearty, full bodied 1962 French Burgundy wine. In the process, I discovered that Bichons on a strict duck and potatoes diet have a very low tolerance for Mexican food. I figured that out when Zac puked in the car after I shared some of my green chili burritos with him. Nancy "asked" that I not do that again.

I actually thought we had the allergies under control, until Zac began scratching again. A friend at work advised us that she found that, Benadryl, an antihistamine designed for humans, helped her dog with allergies. She told us that it made her dog a little drowsy, but did help control the scratching. We tried this with Zac and he did scratch less, mostly because he started sleeping about 23 hours a day.

Right on the heels of the allergy ordeal, Zac came down with a bladder infection. He moped about and complained during urination. This necessitated another trip to the vet for tests and more pills. Did you ever try to take a urine sample from a hyperactive, hypoallergenic, hyper allergenic dog? This was no easy task. Since Zac was neutered not long ago and lost his masculinity, he is especially leery of humans probing around in this area of his body. After viewing my awkward attempts to collect a urine sample, one neighbor considered calling the ASPCA.

No sooner was the bladder infection thing resolved, than it was time for Zac's annual shots. He got the full battery of inoculations including, rabies and distemper. Nancy said sometimes she wished I could get a distemper shot myself. If I'm out of sorts occasionally, it only the results of the dad gum vet bills piling up on my desk.

This is clearly not Zac's favorite time of the year and he comes home from the vet limping and looking pitiful. This year I could commiserate since I had to get all of my shots up to date to go on my mission trip to Vietnam.

This was a story in itself. While in the Air Force, I had to keep all my shots current since we could be called upon to deploy anywhere in the world on a moment's notice. After leaving active duty I had allowed my shot record to get out of date. I wasn't overly concerned about diseases I might contract transiting West Buechel or Pleasure Ridge Park as opposed to some third world area.

I inquired about getting the shots at the clinic downtown where many Southeast short-term mission trip participants get their shots. When I was on active duty, I got my shots for free. This time it was going to be several hundred dollars. After paying all the vet bills, I clearly couldn't afford several hundred dollars on my shots.

While pondering what to do about this situation, Nancy asked why I didn't go to Fort Knox to get my shots. Duh! I had completely forgotten that as a retired veteran I am authorized to use military medical facilities. So off we went to Ft. Knox one morning. Our missions department advised me that I would need shots for Hepatitis A, B, and C (I'm glad there is no Hepatitis D), cholera, Japanese encephalitis (I told them I wasn't going to Japan but they shot me anyway), tetanus, TB tine test, and athlete's foot, I think. It turned out to be 7 shots. The wonderful woman who gave me the shots was, believe it or not, named Fanny, but I told her I wanted the shots in my arm even though it might mess up my golf game the next day.

Once Fanny had finished she put some Band-Aids on my wounds and now I can tell the Army's dirty little secret.

They use Pooh Bear Band-Aids. That's right. The virile, manly, be-all-you-can-be Army uses Pooh Bear Band-Aids. I waited in the clinic areas as instructed, expecting at least a Purple Heart, and finally I went back to work limping and looking as pitiful as a one-year old Bichon after his annual battery of shots. I was explaining my plight to Kristen Evans, Involvement Secretary when, I kid you not, Small Groups Minister, Murphy Belding passed by and greeted me cheerily with a slap my on the arm. After I got up off my knees, I had renewed empathy with my boy Zac.

In fact, I have spiritual ailments similar to Zac's physical ones. Spiritually I am allergic to sin. We all are. Every time I am exposed to it I have an adverse spiritual reaction. From time to time I get infections, too, which cause my spiritual body to get weak and increase the possibility of more serious disease. I have learned that I can avoid allergies and infections by avoiding the places where I am tempted. Another way to prevent serious spiritual disease is to be inoculated against them by immersing myself in God's word, spending time consulting with the Great Physician and attending church regularly to worship and fellowship with other believers.

Life as a granddad is difficult

B efore I begin teaching my ABF class, the Cornerstone, I usually open with a monolog about some relevant event in the church, my life or the headlines. Recently, as I was leaving class one of our class members asked me: "Did you know you spent twice as much time talking about your new dog, Zacchaeus, as you did talking about your grandson. You need to get your priorities straight."

I was immediately convicted by Jim's comment and as I reflected on his observation, he was probably right. We had acquired our new, loveable puppy while our grandson was visiting us for a couple of weeks, and my monologue was disproportionately devoted to my pooch and not my progeny. So let me set the record straight and share with you what I learned during the summer visit of Donald Ellis Waddell, the fifth, my first grandchild.

Lesson 1. Life as a granddad is difficult. Our visit got off to a shaky start when in route from Tallahassee to Louisville, we stopped for lunch just outside of Nashville. Donnie said he wanted a cheeseburger and I took him at his word. When we returned to the car and Don examined his lunch, however, he was perturbed. "Where's my Sponge Bob Square Pants toy with my happy meal?" he asked with tears welling up in his eyes. "You asked for a cheeseburger!" I countered knowing I was in trouble and realizing that the chance of setting a world land speed record from Tallahassee to Louisville was now all but gone. "I'm sorry," I bribed, "next time I'll buy you ten happy meals." While Donnie was temporarily mollified, I knew I had blown any chance I had of being nominated for "Grandfather of the Year."

Lesson 2. You can go the zoo, never see an animal and that's OK. When my kids were about Donnie's age, my parents began taking us to the zoo. It was always a great time that has become something of a family tradition, and now I take my grandkids to the zoo when they come to town. I anticipated sharing with Donnie lengthy, educational explanations of zoology and the wonder of God's creation. Little did I expect that the majority of our time, and my money, would be spent on the merry-go-round, a big inflated air bag that kids bounce on, train rides, standing in line for ice cream, slurpies, and hot dogs. This would have frustrated the life out of me as a parent; as a grandparent it was quality time with my grandson.

Lesson 3. Being a granddad can be a very expensive proposition. I read recently in *USA Today*, that it takes about a quarter of a million dollars to raise a child today. The article didn't estimate the cost of raising a grandkid, but I think it may be greater than a quarter of million when you factor in "Happy Meals" and grandmothers. There were times during his two-week visit that I concluded we should move into Toys-R-Us since we were there so much.

And the trip to the video arcade required us to take out a second mortgage on our house. The person who invented Chuck E. Cheese is a genius. Here is a business that tricks unsuspecting grandparents by taking money, converting it into tokens, which allow the kids to play a 20 second game of some sort that rewards the player paper tickets with which you can redeem for worthless prizes. Genius, pure genius. I am the schlum who forks over hundreds of dollars to keep my grandkids entertained. I can remember when a buck would last all day at Fountain Ferry, the local amusement park. Now a buck gets you four tokens.

Lesson 4. Being short and old is a bummer. Actually, I knew this already but Donnie learned this lesson when we went Kentucky Kingdom. As we purchased our tickets, the ticket lady had Donnie stand next to a measuring stick and determined he was 46 ½ inches tall. "You get in for half price since you're under 48 inches tall," she said, and I was pleased at my good fortune. What I later discovered was that being an inch and a half short of four feet meant that we couldn't go on any of the really cool rides thanks to all the trial lawyers and our litigious society.

Then the ticket lady asked if I were over 55 years of age. "No," I responded automatically but then I remembered that I had just had a birthday the previous month and told her that I was, in fact, 55 years old. "You get in half price, too," she responded. Initially, I was a little bit confused and told her I was over 48 inches tall (perhaps not by much). "It's a senior citizen's discount," she said with too much amusement in her voice to suit me. This was a most traumatic occasion for me: My first senior citizen discount. I thought about declining it but $17 is $17 and I might need that money to pay for the 10 Happy Meals I still owed Donnie.

Lesson 5. You need to stay on your toes while your grandkids are visiting. During Donnie's visit I had to come in on Sunday evening to perform a baptism. I don't use waders when I baptize people and opt to go barefoot into the baptistery like the people I am baptizing. As Donnie, Nancy and I were leaving the house for church that evening, Nancy asked if I had remembered that I had let Donnie paint my toe nails red, white and blue over the 4th of July holiday.

Actually I had forgotten and I suspected that this patriotic display might distract from the spirituality of the baptism, so

Nancy quickly located the nail polish remover and we saved a potentially embarrassing situation. However, I did forget earlier in the week when I disrobed in the men's locker room after my lunchtime run. Embarrassed beyond words, I opted to take a shower with my socks on preferring to be thought of as weird rather than effeminate.

I learned a lot about being a granddad during Donnie's visit. It's expensive, it's tiring but it's more fun than a human being should be allowed to have. No matter what you may hear from the pulpit, my grandsons are the cutest, most intelligent grandchildren east of the Mississippi. Donnie and I have a special relationship, and I look forward to growing even closer in the coming years.

But during his visit, I was reminded of the special responsibility I have to help his parents pass on our faith to Donnie and our other grandchildren. Because grandparents have a special relationship, we can teach them the stories of the Bible and communicate God's love in ways parents can't.

I have learned this as I have listened to hundreds of new members tell their stories during meetings with our pastors. It is uncanny how often, when asked how they came to faith, a new member will site the positive influence of a grandparent had on them as they were growing up. I hope that someday, one of my grandkids will credit me as having a positive influence on their walk with Christ.

It is not good for man to live alone…he might hurt himself

Genesis 2:18 "The LORD God said, "It is not good for the man to be alone."

God was right (of course). It is not good for man to be alone. I pointed that out to my wife, Nancy, as she packed her bags and headed south again to visit our kids and grandkids who live in Tallahassee. "Are you leaving me again?" I asked irritably. She dismissed my protest with a flip of her hand and reminded me that I left her alone a lot during frequent Air Force deployments in my previous life.

How many times do I have to be reminded about the time a Typhoon struck Okinawa while we lived there, and I deserted her and the kids? Actually it wasn't my fault; it was a matter of national security. You see as a pilot my job was to protect the multimillion-dollar jets and somebody had to fly them to the Philippines when the menacing storm began to approach, and it might as well be me. I promised not to have any fun and wished her well as she began boarding up windows and I left to "slip the surly bonds of earth" heading for the tropical paradise.

Back to the present, Nancy gave me that "you've got a lot of making up to do" look, kissed me on the cheek and jumped in our Honda for the 12-hour trip to Tallahassee.

Still, it didn't seem fair to me. I have a full time job evangelizing the lost, edifying the saved, ministering to those in need, being the conscience in the community and meeting newspaper deadlines. More to the point, I have to work overtime so I can continue to support my wife in the extravagant, jet-setting life style to which she has grown accustomed. You know there are child labor laws. There ought to be adult megachurch minister laws, too!

I'm sure Nancy hadn't crossed the Jefferson County line before things began to go wrong at home. The first catastrophe occurred shortly after she left. Our Bichon Frise, Zac, requires allergy shots twice a week for his scratching. (I can't believe I have a dog that requires allergy shots, but that's another story.) Normally, I hold the dog and Nancy administers the shot. Zac is not too cooperative when we poke a sharp needle under his skin, so I have to hold him tightly.

But with Nancy on her way to an all expense paid vacation in Florida, I had to hold the dog and give him the shot by myself. I was confident I could do this and devised a clever plan that involved wrapping Zac's leash around one thigh while draping my other leg over his back. I planned to surprise him with a kind of "hit and run" injection, but the moment he smelled alcohol he began to squirm.

Now if you can imagine this sight: My legs were wrapped like a pretzel around this 15-pound fluffy ball of fur, I pinched the loose skin just behind his neck and thrust the needle quickly and expertly...into my left thumb. At just the wrong moment, Zac bolted to dodge the incoming projectile. Ouch!! The bad news is that my thumb hurt like the dickens. The good news is that I didn't scratch for a week. It is not good for man to be alone.

When Nancy is at home she takes Zac out regularly to perform his necessary bodily functions. However, during a recent visit to the vet for his continued scratching, we were advised to keep him away from grass to mitigate the worst allergies. Excuse me? Isn't that like telling a human to avoid toilets? Anyway, while Nancy is away, Zac's trips outdoors are reduced in number and duration.

Now, Zac is a good dog. He is housebroken and also paper-trained. When Nancy is away I try to go home during lunch to let Zac out. When my duties at church might preclude me coming home, I put down some specially scented papers that you can buy at the pet store for a king's ransom. One day I was particularly busy so I couldn't get home, but it wasn't until I was driving home late that evening that I remembered that I forgot to put his papers down. Whoops! I knew I was going to come home to a mess. But he surprised me and, bless his heart, it appeared he held it for a new indoor world record, 8 hours and 38 minutes!!

I was so impressed and proud of my boy...until Nancy returned home from Florida and went barefoot into our guest bathroom and stepped on the carpet. It squished beneath her feet. It is not good for man to be alone.

Several years ago during one of Nancy's boondoggles to Florida she called me on the phone. You'd think her love for me and compassion for the intolerable position she'd put me in would have prompted the phone call. Not exactly. Her first words were, "Have you remembered to water the plants?" It wasn't exactly a lie when I said "yes." I had remembered at one time...but then I forgot. (I think it was the smoke alarm that diverted my attention at the time but that, too, was another story.)

As I looked at Nancy's favorite, but anemic plant, I doubted it could be saved. Can you do CPR on a plant? Its once perky blooms drooped hopelessly, and the formerly green leaves were a dingy brown. I poured a couple of gallons of water in the pot and said a prayer. Just to be safe I watered all the houseplants, but Nancy later advised me that the others were artificial. Never mind, I thought they looked a lot better after watering.

So this time when Nancy left I was determined that I would not forget to water the plants faithfully. I was so proud of myself. I never missed a watering and the plants flourished. About 10 days after Nancy left, however, I noticed that Zac wasn't needing to go out as much an usual. Hmmm. Then I discovered him sitting expectantly by his water bowl looking up at me with sad puppy dog eyes. I slapped my forehead with the palm of my hand. "You idiot," I said to myself, "you forgot to water the dog." It's not good for man to be alone.

Zac looked at me as if to say, "It's not good for a dog to be alone with a man who lives alone."

Zac on steroids, move over Hulk Hogan

Actually I liked Zac better with ears. Zacchaeus is our two-year-old Bichon Frise who I write about from time to time. No, he didn't have an "earlebotamy," but he did have a close encounter, make that a very close encounter with his beautician. Some refer to the person who cuts a dog's hair as a groomer, but I call her a beautician just to irritate Zac. It's all very unmanly but then again, a white curly haired emasculated canine probably isn't ever going to be too manly under any circumstances. I mean, we're not talking pit bull here.

But the reason Zac had all the hair on his ears cut off is kind of a long story. The executive summary is this: Zac has allergies. Now this doesn't make sense to me. One of the reasons we bought a Bichon Frise puppy was that they are hypoallergenic. That means that they don't cause an allergic reaction in humans. But while they don't give allergies that doesn't mean they don't get them. And, since this causes him to be sick quite often that sort of makes Zac a hypoallergenic, hyper allergenic, hyperactive, hypochondriac.

So, Zac had an ear infection due to his allergies. The vet prescribed eardrops in addition to antibiotics that were so expensive we had to go to Canada to get them. The eardrops had a pernicious, unexpected consequence. The excess drops seeped out and matted the hair around his ears.

Nancy asked Zac's groomer (who charges more to cut Zac's hair than Nancy's "groomer" charges to cut hers) to cut out the mats and "even up the ears." The result was shocking. Nancy tried to prepare me when I called her on the way home, but the naked truth was Zac had no ears. In removing the mats and attempting to even up the ears, the groomer had removed all the hair leaving our puppy looking like a cross between Yul Bruner and a hairless Chihuahua.

Phase two of the plan to combat Zac's allergies was to put him on steroids. Zac on steroids is not a pretty sight. When I think of steroid use I visualize a bemuscled, 275-pound linebacker in the NFL stomping the faces of running backs into the ground. I do not visualize a two-year-old, 12-pound Bichon Frise. So when the vet said we had to put Zac on steroids to alleviate his scratching, I thought he was kidding. Aren't dogs supposed to scratch? Isn't that what dogs do? All this led to an overnight stay at the vet for observation. It would have been cheaper to check both Zac and the vet into a four-star hotel. Regardless, the steroids didn't work.

One day I came home after a tough day of saving souls and being the conscience of the community, and Nancy reported her conversation with Zac's allergist. "Let's stop right there," I demanded. "Are you telling me we have an allergist for our mutt?" I mean, I was going broke just paying the vet bills, now we have a specialist to tend to the scratching.

But the steroids, transformed our boy from a playful puppy into an aggressive, occasionally obnoxious eating machine. You've heard of barking at the moon? Zac barked furiously at his food dish. Really. And I'm sure Zac didn't understand why he was perpetually hungry. So now Zac eats everything in sight---golf tees, Kleenex (kind of like toilet paper from the inside out, I suppose), pens. What he doesn't eat, he licks for latent food value.

When the steroids didn't stop the scratching, we began the allergy tests. He was sensitive to pollen allergens, mold and dust mites. We were told to restrict his outdoor time. But the test revealed that he was especially sensitive to grain mites. Actually, I didn't know there was such a thing as a grain mite. So, we had to switch from dry dog food to stinky canned dog food.

In any event the steroids didn't do the trick, so Zac's allergists (I can't believe I'm admitting this in public) told us we'd have to start giving him allergy shots. Now, we're kind of used to shots around our house. Nancy has been taking Beta Seron shots for her MS for almost 10 years, and I have administered a good number of these shots since the site of shot location is inaccessible for Nancy unless she were to sit on the needle.

There was an instruction sheet that accompanied the allergy shots that contained a list of warnings, precautions that rivaled any legalese I'd seen on a human medication. (Written by literal legal beagles, perhaps?)

One warning was to observe your pet for at least one hour after injection. Zac lapses into depression if we neglect him for 5 minutes. He is under constant surveillance. The original lap dog, he is invariably ensconced on Nancy's lap.

A second warning was that a small amount of redness and itchiness may be seen at the site of the injection. Wait a minute. I thought we were giving the dad gum shots to eliminate itching, not cause it.

"If your pet becomes very itchy after an injection," the instructions continued, "or shows any signs of hives, weakness, vomiting, diarrhea, pale gums or difficulty breathing--call your veterinarian immediately." Maybe I over reacted but I called the vet. The receptionist advised us that he was vacationing in the Cayman Islands. Apparently he had come into a large windfall about 2 years ago when he had taken on a new patient. "Wasn't it 2 years ago that we started taking Zac to see our vet?" I asked Nancy.

Eventually we got the following diagnosis from our vet: "The diagnosis of allergy consists of a thorough examination, correlated with a carefully taken history, and evaluation of appropriate differential diagnoses. The definitive diagnosis is supported by in vitro tests for allergen-specific IgE or in vivo tests (intradermal skin tests) the results of which are used in the formulation of immunotherapy. When allergy occurs, the clinical manifestations are that of atopic dermatitis (local or generalized), urticaria, otitis, blepharitis and rarely asthma." A rough translation of this medical jargon is: Dogs scratch, but this is going to cost you big bucks, sucker.

Nancy's hairdresser said she thought Zac was costing us too much money and needed to be put down. I was stunned at the suggestion. I mean, I'm not necessarily an animal rights type of guy, but I've grown kind of fond of the little blighter. Besides what would I have to write about without Zac?

Just when I thought our obsession with our pets couldn't get any zanier; I read an article about Canine Dental Care in *Dog Fancy* magazine while I was waiting in the vet for Zac to be seen. It read: "Your pooch can get braces. Experts say good dental care could add years to your pet's life." At the current rate of vet bills, I'm not sure we can afford for him to live too many years beyond his normal life expectancy, so I hid the braces article so Zac and his mom couldn't see it.

If God's your co-pilot, change seats

I had lunch with Steve Pollock, a good friend and New Member Ministry volunteer. Some time ago, he shared with me his pride over his son Adam soloing in the T-38 in Air Force pilot training. The story made me nostalgic for my pilot training days over 40 years ago.

I remembered when I soloed for the first time. It was a cool, dry day in late February in Big Spring, Texas. There was the smell of the flight line in my nostrils, the ubiquitous aroma of aviation fuel and the asphalt tarmac.

I had mixed feelings as I headed for my aircraft. Yes, I was nervous at the thought of being airborne with someone as inexperienced as I at the controls. I was also a bit embarrassed. You see my diminutive stature required me to take a pillow along in flight to assist me in reaching the rudder pedals (a really important thing when flying). In any event, it's hard to strut to your aircraft with visions of becoming a "studly" fighter pilot while carrying a Serta sleep-tight pillow under your arm. Still I was excited at the prospects of becoming a pilot and flying by myself for the first time.

I looked briefly in my rear view mirror as I lifted off and watched the runway disappear behind me. My airspeed increased through 90 knots, and the altimeter showed a slow but steady ascent. I was airborne by myself for the first time piloting the T-41, the Air Force equivalent of the Cessna 172, a single engine propeller aircraft that seats four.

There were four seats in the aircraft but only one was occupied that day. The empty seat was normally occupied by my instructor pilot, who had written the words "cleared solo" in my grade book and waited on the ground for my return.

Once airborne, I started hearing noises from the engine I hadn't noticed before. The turbulence seemed greater than I had experienced when my instructor pilot was seated next to me. What would I do if the engine quit? Where would I land? What if I got lost?

My first solo flight as an Air Force pilot was completed without incident, but in the process I learned at least one important lesson about my Christian walk, and that is that we are never flying solo. The promised Holy Spirit and faithful Christian friends are always with us to guide and comfort us.

When we accept Christ, we are forever God's adopted children. When I gave my life to Christ in 1954, God became my Heavenly father and I became His son. Many times in my adult life I thought I was on my own, flying solo. I now know He was there all the time. He was in control.

As the Psalmist wrote in 139:7-10: "Where can I go from your Spirit? Where can I flee from your presence? If I go up to the heavens, you are there; if I make my bed in the depths, you are there. If I rise on the wings of the dawn, if I settle on the far side of the sea, even there your hand will guide me, your right hand will hold me fast." In John 14:16-18 Jesus promises us the Holy Spirit to be with us forever. In Hebrews 13:5 we find that He will never leave or forsake us.

As His children, God loves us even when we wander away and get off-course. He is wanting us back, wooing us back to Him, a process poignantly portrayed in the Parable of the Prodigal Son. I see this so clearly now at various points in my life. When I was deeply absorbed in my career and worldly pleasures and pursuits, He was sending people in my life to remind me of my relationship with Him.

I think of Mildred McFall who compelled me to teach Sunday School when I thought I would be too busy with my pilot training studies. I think of our good friend Betty Brown who was patiently teaching me the meaning of grace, while I was supposed to be teaching her in a home Bible study at our house. When I was tempted to misbehave and act like a fighter pilot, He sent other Christians like Terry and Judy Boswell to help me return to the paths of righteousness. When I needed to be discipled and challenged to grow in my faith, He sent Ron Furgerson and Cecil McGee.

Just like my first solo flight in February 1970, I thought I was on my own in life, but He was in the right seat taking the controls of my life when I was headed for a spiritual mishap. Many years ago I read an interesting book, *God is My Copilot*, by Colonel Robert L. Scott. I don't recall it being a particularly spiritual book and as I have grown in my faith, I'm not sure I like the title, now that I think about it. I'm more inclined now to agree with the bumper sticker I saw some years ago which said: "If God is your copilot, change seats."

God isn't my copilot. I have come to think of him as my perpetual Instructor Pilot who never leaves me, even when I think I'm flying solo.

Our Florida vacation: Heaven except for the tropical storm

Any Florida vacation that begins with a tropical storm is off to a turbulent start. I suppose it was my fault since I am the one who scheduled the trip in the first place, made the reservations and paid for the hotel rooms. But there we were, rolling into Panama City while Tropical Storm Bill was making landfall in New Orleans and spreading its winds and rain up into the panhandle of Florida.

We were meeting my cousins, Frank, Don and Gerry Wilder and their families for a week's vacation as we had for many years. Our vacations together date back 52 years when my dad and mom would rendezvous with his sister, Elizabeth, and her husband Frank. Often our parents would rent one house for the entire clan. More recently, the Wilders had purchased beachfront condos, and we tagged along staying in a nearby hotel.

Our usual vacation bill of fare consists of golf, fishing, playing in the waves, spending copious quantities of my money and just hanging around and relaxing. But it almost goes without saying that a tropical storm changes that scenario significantly. Since I was unprepared for this eventuality, I'd like to share with you some helpful hints in the form of my "Top ten things to do during a tropical storm in Florida" just in case you find yourself in a similar predicament some day.

Activity 10) Since the surf is up and red flags are flying, you're not going to get in the water so you might try some other forms of surfing. Surfing the Internet is good. It's kind of like hanging ten on a keyboard instead of a surfboard. Channel surfing is another option, but by Wednesday I had already worn out two remotes and was experiencing early symptoms of carpal tunnel syndrome in my right hand.

Activity 9) Go to the movies. Initially this sounded like a great idea! But guess what? Everyone else in northern Florida had the same idea at the same time. We all converged on the same theater at the same time in the midst of a deluge that was reminiscent of Noah and the flood. "Granddad," my family said in unison, "you stand in line while we go shopping."

I couldn't have gotten wetter if I had gone swimming in the Gulf, except swimming was forbidden due to the sea state; and of course, that was the reason I was standing in line at the movie theater, rain dripping from the bill of my ball cap and sneakers filling up with water. Then I spent half my life standing in line for refreshments that required a Kings' Ransom to pay for.

I got to go with my youngest grandson, while everyone else saw an adult movie. There were only two PG movies on the schedule that day, and he had seen both 17 times. I think we watched "The Return of Elmo," but I'm not absolutely sure. I dozed off twice only to be awakened by the sound effects emanating from the speakers. Of course we had to sit on the front row and I left the theater with a permanent crick in my neck.

Activity 8) Watch your grandsons play. This is great sport, not unlike Friday Night Fights on ESPN. It begins innocently enough with each playing in their own area with their own toys. Then there is gradual escalation, words, touching, pushing, followed by full-scale combat. "Make him stop!" "I'm not doing anything." "I hate you." This continues until a parent (not granddad) intercedes and initiates a cease-fire, which lasts about as long as an Israeli-Palestinian peace accord.

Activity 7) Work a crossword puzzle. This is always a good choice. Of course there is renewed interest in crossword puzzles since doctors now tell us that working crossword puzzles may help prevent Alzheimer's disease. Oh great, my mental health may depend on me knowing a four-letter word for a Roman word.

Activity 6) Tease your pregnant daughter-in-law about negotiating the narrow steps into the second floor loft. If looks could kill, I would be a dead man.

Activity 5) Eat. Take a nap. Eat. Take a nap. My wife's routine prompted my 4-year old grandson, Devin, to remark. "Grandma, all you do is eat and sleep." To wit, Nancy replied, "And your point would be?"

Activity 4) Play games. To be honest, if I have to play another hand of Old Maid, I think I'll "Go Fish." Still, the kid games at least had a beginning and an end. Some of the games my kids brought along lasted forever.

Activity 3) Go shopping. This is similar to going to the movies (everyone in Northern Florida is crowding into the mall) except a lot more expensive. Nancy can spend incredible amounts of cash when our grandkids are hundreds of miles away. When Donnie, Devin and Erin are coaching her, her will power evaporates, the word "no" vanishes from her vocabulary, and we have to let the Visa card cool down for several days before using it again.

Going shopping is almost as expensive as going to the amusement park and enjoying the indoor activities. These consist mostly of games where you put money in a vending machine that converts money into tokens that you put into games that convert the tokens into paper tickets that you can redeem for worthless prizes. Whoever invents this scheme is a diabolical genius who is now retired to an island in the Caribbean. I hope his home is hit be a tropical storm, and he loses everything.

2) Just enjoy the fellowship. Being relationally challenged, this is tough for me. I mean, I like fellowship, but just in small quantities. I'm a pretty typical type A clod who likes to be doing a lot of things. I don't say that with any pride, and I'm trying to do better in my relationship with Christ and with others, but my idea of a perfect vacation is every day planned to the minute with lots of entertaining activities. In the past, I had made almost everyone miserable with my tightly compressed itineraries. Then I get impatient when things don't go exactly as planned. This is a difficult posture to maintain in the midst of a tropical storm.

So we spent a lot of time with each other doing nothing in particular. As we sat on the beach one afternoon during a brief respite from the rain, I truly enjoyed just relaxing and chatting. I watched grandkids and cousins playing with each other. The Wilder brothers were chatting, and it was clear they enjoy each other's company. They were brothers but they were also friends. I marveled at the closeness of their relationship.

Out of the Waddell and Wilder families represented there, I counted 10 kids and 19 grandkids. When you throw in my parents and my aunt and uncle Wilder (now deceased) that's a whole lot of close-knit families without a single divorce among them. I was amazed. Don and Doris Waddell and Frank and Elizabeth Wilder had done a great job of modeling what a family should be.

Ravi Zacharias, the Indian born, Cambridge educated apologist of the Christian faith said, "A key to understanding the nature of God is found in relationships." I witnessed that in these families and was left wondering if I didn't also get a glimpse of heaven in the process. That is heaven, minus the tropical storm.

Activity 1) And the number one thing to do during a tropical storm on your Florida vacation...write an *Outlook* article about what you did during your Florida vacation.

There ought to be a law against grandpa abandonment

Nancy left me for a younger man...again. Actually, she deserted me for three younger men, our grandsons who live in Tallahassee. I think it's great she wants to be an integral part of our grandkids growing up years, but where's the love around my house. I have needs, too.

Anyway, Nancy left me alone to take care of Zac, the house and, oh by the way, earn a living so I can continue to support her in the extravagant, jet-setting (or in this case, Honda Accord-setting) life style to which she has grown accustomed. I'm sure she hadn't gotten to the city limits when things started to unravel at home.

First, Zac doesn't adjust well to his mom being away. His toilet habits are the biggest challenge, even without the emotional stress of living alone with me. Basically he's used to going outside every four hours, while my boss is used to me working at least twice that long. While I was willing to come home for lunch, I knew there would be times he'd be alone for extended periods. Through trial and error (mostly error), we have learned that he can go 5 ½ hours between potty breaks.

Unfortunately, I came home from work after 5 ¾ hours. Initially I thought he had not made a mess, and praised him for his bladder and bowel control. He looked at me curiously as if to say, "I wonder if these humans discuss their toilet habits as much as they talk about mine." Later that evening I discovered his indiscretion when I was washing the dishes in my stocking feet. At first I felt only dampness and assumed I had slopped some water onto the mat on the floor. Soon my socks were soaked and it dawned on me what I was standing in. Zac! We had paper-trained him as a puppy and I had to admit that the kitchen mat looked a lot like his puppy pads we used.

Maybe he was still angry with me for trying to starve him. Nancy had emphasized that I should change his water every other day and feed him daily. I think I got the watering and feeding intervals mixed up. My mistake was brought to my attention when I discovered my emaciated pup barking at his empty bowl.

Then there was the problem with the laundry. Normally I just sort of let the dirty clothes accumulate until Nancy returns. But this time she was gone longer than normal, and I was having a difficult time getting the laundry room door open. So I set about to do the clothes. I don't think washing clothes should be that complicated, and it should be within my intellectual capabilities---I mean I have an advance degree from an accredited university. I've flown sophisticated supersonic aircraft. But washing clothes is so confusing. You have to separate the dark and light clothes. Do I use bleach? There are several varieties of soap to choose from and a bewildering array of dials and settings on the washer control panel.

But after a week I was facing a crisis. I ran out of underwear half way through my ordeal. Either I had to wash a load or go to the store and buy some new skivvies. I took the easy way out and later that day I made my way to Walmart for some fresh Fruit of the Looms.

During her absence, my eating habits change dramatically. I'm now on a first name basis with all the fast food cashiers in the local area. When forced to eat at home I exist on a staple of hotdogs and Pop Tarts. I have a great recipe for hotdogs, by the way, which I will give you if you like. I can take a hotdog from frozen to consumed in six minutes and thirty-five seconds. They're not much to look at with the exploded ends and the flavor leaves something to be desired unless you really like mustard and relish, but it's a three course dinner (i.e. one hot dog per course) that is quick and practical, if not particularly nutritious. I balance my diet with healthy servings of ice cream and nachos (the jalapeños count as a vegetable).

Then I faced another crisis: I ran out of hot dogs less than a week after Nancy's departure. Fortunately, two members of my Cornerstone ABF, Burch and O'Neal Moberly, came to my rescue. Moved by compassion, they invited me over at the last minute to their "Dinners for Eight." (Dinner for Eight is a program in ABF classes where eight class members meet and eat at the home of a member.) I like the last minute invitation because no one expects you to bring anything. Given my menu of Pop Tarts and hot dogs, however, I don't know that anyone was particularly anxious for me to bring anything anyway.

Despite my travails, I believe Nancy is wise to be committed to being a strong influence in the lives of our grandkids. Our children and their wives are committed Christians, but Nancy is going to do her part to help these boys grow up in the "nurture and admonition of the Lord" as the Paul advised parents in the King James version of Ephesians 6:4. If our grandkids are to survive with our faith deeply held within their hearts, we need to help their parents by prayer and encouragement.

When Nancy reads a story about Jesus to our grandkids, Donnie, Devin, Amy or Erin, she's helping in this process. When she talks about her faith in God, they pay particular attention because it's grandma who is saying it. Parents just can't have the same influence because they are regarded differently.

I listened to Nancy Ortberg when she spoke here during the North American Christian Convention several years ago. She told of her own walk with the Lord that began at the feet of her grandmother who loved her and told her about Jesus and had such a profound influence on her that Nancy grew up committed to the Lord and now serves in the ministry. My Nancy is doing the same thing, and I guess it's OK if I have to fend for myself occasionally surviving on hotdogs and Pop Tarts.

Black Friday at Toys R Us, and other mental disorders

You know, there's nothing like Christmas shopping to take the Christmas spirit out of Christmas. I was reminded of this truism several years ago when I found myself in line at Toys R Us the day after Thanksgiving. "What on earth am I doing here on Black Friday?" I thought to myself.

During the Thanksgiving holiday our sons, their wives and our grandchildren make their annual pilgrimage to Louisville from Tallahassee. We then go to Boston, Kentucky to enjoy our traditional Thanksgiving meal with Nancy's relatives.

With the obligatory functions completed on Thursday, I then began to seriously consider what I would do to entertain my grandkids on the day after Thanksgiving while their parents were shopping. As far as I was concerned, shopping was not even a remote possibility...or so I thought. "How about going to the public library?" I suggested to my grandkids. This was greeted with the anticipated distain. "How about the art museum?" My namesake, Donald Ellis Waddell the 5th, folded his arms defiantly and squinting slightly said emphatically: "I want to go to Toy's R Us!" "Toys R Us, Toys R Us" the kids began to chant in unison.

So we piled into the car and headed down Shelbyville Road with the first strains of Christmas carols being heard on the radio. I was humming "Peace on Earth, Good Will Toward Men" as we turned onto Shelbyville Road in front of the Mall only to discover that the six lane highway I remembered the day before had been transformed into a parking lot overnight.

We survived the trip to the Toys R Us parking lot but there were several terrifying near misses in route that made flying combat in Vietnam seem like child's play (so to speak) by comparison. After considerable searching, I finally found a parking spot but I could barely see the store in the distance. As we entered the store I explained that each grandson could spend $10 on a maximum of three toys. I had already done the math and knew that we could use the express checkout line with 9 items.

Nancy took Don the 5th to look for a specialized plaything while Devin and Erin went with me and each selected a set of handcuffs, Sheriff's badge and a brightly colored flashlight that made a shrill, annoying siren-like sound. I was almost gleeful at the thought of how much the noisemaker was going to annoy Devin and Erin's parents.

Even though my wife, Nancy, was lost in the teeming masses of Black Friday shoppers, I was delighted that my ordeal might soon be over and Erin, Devin and I headed for the express checkout line with "peace on earth, good will toward men" still ringing in my ears.

Somewhere between selecting the final toy and taking my place in the checkout line my attitude took a decided turn for the worse. The express line (limit of 10 items) was several blocks long, and I reflexively counted the number of items in the baskets in front of me. We were OK, too. Erin and Devin had six items. Donnie's three would keep us one under the limit when Nancy rendezvoused with us, an event I had carefully timed to correspond to our arrival at the cash register.

The "express" line was moving excruciatingly slow. Two ladies almost got into a fistfight jockeying for position. Another lady was apparently traumatized by the furor and was staring blankly off into space in a semi-comatose state. "Peace on earth, good will toward men" I reminded myself. This time the refrain was more in the form of a question.

I began to chat with the lady in front of me, and we lamented the long line and wondered why we were so stupid as to be shopping on Black Friday. We got to know each other pretty well in the ensuing hours of waiting and agreed to add each other to our Christmas card mailing list.

Our conversation was interrupted by several kids in an adjacent line who began crying, presumably because they were not getting what they wanted. A mother lashed out at an uncooperative toddler. Another lady sighed audibly as she crossed several items off her shopping list that still remained very long I was almost at the cash register when Nancy and Donnie showed up. Instead of three items we agreed to, they had five. That put us over the limit, and I felt like all eyes were glaring at me. I hastily put my hand over the logo on my Southeast windbreaker. Finally, I glanced nervously at the ladies waiting in line behind me and forcing a smile said: "Peace on earth, good will toward _men_."

As I stood in the line immersed in the hustle and bustle of Black Friday, I wondered if we hadn't missed the point; if we hadn't perverted the most blessed event in the history of civilization and converted it into an affair that achieves exactly the opposite of "peace on earth, good will to men." I resolved as much as possible to put the Christ back in Christmas this season.

The traumatic Thanksgiving in Tallahassee

Let me tell you about my traumatic Thanksgiving in Tallahassee. Normally, our boys, Don and David, bring their families to visit us for Thanksgiving and then Nancy and I go to Tallahassee for Christmas. This year however Don's wife, Tammy, was still dealing with some health issues and David and his wife Rae were new parents and didn't want to make the long trip to Kentucky and back. So Nancy and I headed south this year unaware of the travails that awaited.

Now, when I was a colonel in the Air Force I always got a room by myself when I traveled and later as a wing commander usually stayed in the VIP suite. As a granddad staying with my kids, I got the upper bunk. It's kind of like the VIP suite except different. Very different. My brother and I used to share bunk beds when we were growing up, but I don't recall it being so difficult getting in and out of the upper bunk. Trying to get up in the morning without waking my two grandsons and wife (who was sleeping below) was almost impossible, if for no other reason than my knees creaked audibly, and I groaned involuntarily with each step down.

I went to the pantry to get something to eat and found an impressive array of breakfast cereals, but search as I might I couldn't find any Cheerios, Wheaties or Rice Krispies, the staple of a my diet growing up in the 1950s. It seemed like everything in the pantry was called uninviting names like "Howling Apple Jacks" and "Green Slime." The least offensive product I saw was a box of "Freaky Froot Loops."

I took the box into the family room to watch the morning news, but by the time 7-year old grandson Erin woke up I was stunned to find I had eaten the whole box. Not only had I consumed a week's worth of calories in one sitting, but as I went into the bedroom to change clothes I heard Erin, now standing in front of the pantry say with a tears welling up in his eyes, "Where are my Freaky Froot Loops?" Whoops.

When we arrived in Florida I was on the mend from a pernicious cold and had taken my cough medicine with me. Ever the cautious one when surrounded by young people, I was careful to put my medicine up where the kids couldn't reach it. Erin was also suffering from a cold and Rae, who was nursing Amy, asked Nancy to give Erin his cough medicine. Nancy reached absent-mindedly for the closest bottle and gave Erin an adult dose of my cough medicine. Discovering her mistake, she then gave him a children's dose of his cough medicine. The bad news was that Erin was a little wired for the next few hours. The good news is that he didn't cough for a week. Of course you know who got blamed for the mistake.

Then there was the toothpaste debacle. I shared a bathroom with the kids when we stayed at Donnie and Tammy's house. Back when I was a kid we had <u>bars</u> of soap and <u>tubes</u> of toothpaste. Now everything comes in a dispenser. I should have noticed the difference, but the "Bubble Gum" toothpaste dispenser and the "Very Berry Buzz Lightyear" soft soap dispenser looked a lot alike; especially to a sleepy-eyed granddad whose vision isn't what it used to be. Yuck! I remember my parents washing my mouth out with soap one time, but this time I hadn't said any bad words (although I was tempted to swear after I had the soap in my mouth.)

I also had an Art Linkletter experience during my visit. You remember he hosted a TV program called "Kids Say the Darndest Things." Donnie (8), Devin (5) and I were on the way to Walmart to get some supplies for a school project. Of course, Donnie, like all my grandkids is extremely intelligent. After teaching a class on our culture at Southeast and learning how messed up some of our public schools are, I was questioning Donnie to see what he was learning in school.

I asked about Thanksgiving and the Iraq War. Then, probing into more sensitive cultural issues I asked, "What do you know about homosexuality?" Picking up on the last syllable of the word, Donnie responded, "I don't know, ask my parents." Just a little embarrassed, I clarified emphasizing the first syllable, "No, homosexuality." "You mean people without homes," he teased. "Oh, you mean gays," Donnie offered with apparent sincerity. "We learn about that next year." I was going to ask him about stem research, but I had already learned more than I wanted to know.

So much for my traumatic Thanksgiving in Tallahassee. Despite the travails of our visit, it was worthwhile just to meet our new granddaughter, Amy Nichole Waddell, the first girl born into the Waddell family in 80 years. As I held her, I was amazed at the miracle of God's creation. But she appeared so fragile, innocent and vulnerable. I was apprehensive about her future growing up in a sinful world that seems much more dangerous to kids and to Christians than the world I grew up in.

At the same time, I was encouraged that Amy and all our grandkids were going to grow up in Christian homes where the love of Christ will be learned and seen. I recommitted myself to making sure that grandma and grandpa did their part to "bring them up in the training and instruction of the Lord."

Actually, "after further review" the Thanksgiving visit wasn't so traumatic after all, and it served as a reminder that I have much to be thankful for, not the least of which is our family and the love we share.

Caution: Reading warning labels can be hazardous to your health

"To whom can I speak and give warning? Who will listen to me? Their ears are closed so they cannot hear. The word of the LORD is offensive to them; they find no pleasure in it." Jeremiah 6:10

During our vacation to Gatlinburg this year our nine-month-old granddaughter, Amy Nicole, came along to keep grandma from getting bored. She's not yet walking but gets around pretty well in a walker. Nancy and I examined this device with some amusement comparing it to the walker our son Don used when he was Amy's age. Amy's walker was state of the art and designed to protect her during any potential catastrophe, including nuclear war.

Don's first walker was pitiful by comparison, but it did seem to get the job done. His walker consisted of a flimsy frame with rickety wheels and a seat made of imitation tiger skin cloth. We called him "tiger" and he used the walker like one. Often he'd lose his balance and fall, and mom would set him aright with a "oh, poor darling" or dad would look at his future NFL running back, laugh and say "shake it off and get back up."

Unlike Don's walker, I think Amy's was made of titanium alloy and high impact plastic. It was surely designed by a team of NASA engineers to be indestructible, and the wheelbase was wide enough that it wouldn't turnover in an earthquake. Despite all the safety features however, the walker displayed a large placard containing over a dozen warnings and hazards, enough dire cautions to scare a grandparent witless.

One warning label depicted a walker tumbling down the stairs. It said "Warning Stair Hazard! Avoid serious injury or death. Block stairs securely before using." I thought to myself, "it's a wonder our kids survived without the benefit of such warnings." But there was another, larger placard that warned of many more dire consequences, if the product wasn't used properly. This checklist was an abbreviated course in effective parenting.

It read in part: "Always keep the child in view. Never carry the child in the walker." The walker itself weighed a ton so I didn't think this was a realistic possibility for anyone except a WWF wrestler. The warning labels continued, "To avoid burn injuries always keep child away from hot liquids, radiators, space heaters, fire place or active volcanoes (actually I made up the volcanoes part.) "To avoid drowning never use around swimming pools or bathtubs." All that was missing on the placard was the 1-800 number for a personal injury lawyer.

Now, don't get me wrong. I want my granddaughter to live in a safe environment, but I do not believe that posting a lengthy list of warnings contributes to her safety in any meaningful way. Providing a safe environment for our kids is a parent's job, and I think to a certain extent we have subtly shifted the responsibility away from parents and to an anonymous, unaccountable government agency.

But baby walkers aren't the only product that has warning labels attached to absolve the manufacturer from liability. Have you ever wondered what those little warning labels on the back of NFL player's helmets say? I have. If I were writing the labels they would say something akin to "Warning: If you are stupid enough to play this brutal game with 300 pound Neanderthals who would like nothing better than to rip your head from your shoulders, you deserve whatever you get." In reality, I'm sure this little one by two inch piece of plastic fine print contains the collective wisdom of centuries of civil litigation in an attempt to absolve the manufacturer of any wrong doing or negligence.

Warning labels are becoming an increasingly prominent part of our "lawsuit crazed" society. You remember the lady who got a cup of hot coffee from the drive-through at McDonalds and placed it between her legs when she drove off. When the hot coffee spilled in her lap and burned her badly, she was quick to sue the franchise for not telling her that hot coffee is hot, and if you put a cup on your lap while driving you might burn yourself.

I am sad to report that the lady won a large settlement. Recently when I bought a cup of coffee, it had a warning label on the top which says "Caution: Contents Hot." On the side the message read, "To our valued customer, please be careful. This beverage is extremely hot." I burned my lip anyway...but not my groin! You can be sure I'm not going to sue to let everyone know how stupid I am.

Warnings are everywhere. I was tickled by one I read about which was posted at a convent in California. It read "Warning. No trespassing. Violators will be prosecuted to the full extent of the law. Signed, Sisters of Mercy." The first warnings labels I remember were on cigarettes and said "Smoking has been shown to cause cancer in lab rats." I always thought this was curious since rats can't read and I've never seen one smoke.

In the flying business we had lots of warnings associated with operating supersonic fighters. We were warned on everything from flying too fast or too slow; too high or too low. Only a fighter pilot would have to be warned: "Do not intentionally place this aircraft in uncontrolled flight" or that: "Ejecting at supersonic speed may produce extreme flailing, dismemberment and death."

I'm not opposed to all warning labels, however. I've had warning labels affixed to Nancy's credit cards which say: "Warning: Excessive use of this device may be hazardous to my wealth."

We have some signs around the church designed to prevent damage to property or injury. No parking signs fall into this category. I heard of a church that was considering a new warning to be printed in the bulletin when their elderly pastor was preaching. It would read: "The sermon today may cause drowsiness. Do not operate heavy machinery or vehicles during the service."

All this got me to thinking. What if God placed warning labels on dangerous items? Perhaps a label would be prominently displayed on the front cover of a *Playboy* magazine: "Warning: Continued use of this product may lead to sin and eternal damnation." Maybe God would put a warning label on the forehead of some flirtatious co-worker, which said: "Extremely dangerous. Keep at least 10 feet away at all times." A bottle of booze might contain a warning similar to "Excessive use of this product may result in your burning in Hell for all eternity."

Of course that's all nonsense. Sensible parents don't need warning labels to protect their children in walkers, and Christians don't need visible reminders of the dangers of sin. God's law is clearly set forth in His word and all we have to do is read it and obey.

James 1:22 "Do not merely listen to the word, and so deceive yourselves. Do what it says."

My worst Christmas

*"When they had gone, an angel of the Lord
appeared to Joseph in a dream. "Get up," he said,
"take the child and his mother and escape to Egypt.
Stay there until I tell you, for Herod is going to
search for the child to kill him." Matthew 2:13*

It was December 22, 1971. I was a month or so into a
combat tour as an F-4 fighter pilot stationed in DaNang,
Vietnam where I was a member of the 390th Tactical Fighter
Squadron, a unit with a rich combat history dating back to
World War II.

The squadron scheduling board was a prominent feature of the operations building where we spent most of our
time. The scheduling board was the object of considerable
personal interest since this 6 by 12-foot piece of Plexiglas
revealed our fates each day. We all wanted our name to
appear on the schedule because fighter pilots live to fly. At
the same time, if the sortie was to a high threat area, the
scheduling board postings could increase the heart rate and
anxiety level considerably.

Actually, flying in Vietnam was not excessively dangerous for the most part. Though trips north of the DMZ

had claimed their share of killed or captured, the loss rate wasn't too high on balance. Still, when you saw "Route Pack 6" (a mission in the vicinity of Hanoi) you knew the risk was higher than normal and your heart beat a little faster. Of course, the conventional fighter pilot would never admit any emotion and would declare with unbridled bravado something to the effect of "Bad day for 'Uncle Ho' (Ho Chi Minh, ruler of North Vietnam at the time), I'll be gunning for his best fighter jocks tomorrow."

But today's schedule didn't have any bad news for Uncle Ho or for me. I was scheduled for a night gunship escort in Laos. Escorting the AC-130 Hercules with their sophisticated sensors and rapid firing, accurate guns was an interesting, if not hazardous mission. The AC-130s reconnoitered the Ho Chi Minh trail using their low level light TVs and when finding enemy trucks laden with weapons would open up with 20mm and 40mm computer aimed guns.

Our mission was to orbit above the gunship and bomb antiaircraft artillery positions when they shot at the Hercules. While the AC-130 was deadly accurate, the chances of the Vietnamese gunners hitting the Hercules was nil (none were ever lost to AAA though one did go down to a SAM late in the war), and the chances we'd hit the gun positions at night weren't much better. Our job was to keep their heads down. Each night was a veritable fireworks show with tracers streaming skyward toward the sound of the Hercules, secondary explosions when the AC-130 guns found their target and the dramatic flash of our ordnance dropping on or near gun positions.

In addition to my name next to the words "Gunship Escort," the scheduling board contained a neatly lettered notice that said: "Three more bombing days until Christmas." Actually, I did need to be reminded that Christmas was only a few days away. There was nothing else to put me in the mood. Surely there was no snow; this was the hottest time of the year in Vietnam. This was a strange country in an unfamiliar part of the world, and while the French colonialists left some Christian traditions when they departed, it was definitely not beginning to look a lot like Christmas around the DaNang community. There was no holly, fat men with beards, elves, or stocking hung by the chimney with care. Come to think of it there wasn't even a chimney in the steamy jungles of Vietnam.

As I considered my situation five days before Christmas, I was overcome with sadness. This would be my first Christmas away from family. Everyone I loved was in Louisville, Kentucky---my parents and in-laws were there. So were Nancy and our two boys, Don the 4th, three-years-old and David who had celebrated his first birthday a week earlier without his dad to help him blow out the candle on his cake.

That evening I sought to ease my sadness by calling Nancy. This, however, was a tricky process. In 1971, there was no such thing as an AT&T calling card and long distance phone calls half way around the world could put a healthy dent in a week's paycheck. For this reason, many of us resorted to using the MARS system. MARS stood for "Military Auxiliary Radio System" and required us to call a local HAM radio operator who would contact another HAM radio operator in the vicinity of our family in the U.S. and make the appropriate phone contact.

When I talked over the phone, the MARS operator pushed the transmit button on his radio set and half way around the world Nancy would hear me through the crackle and pop of an atmospheric radio transmission bounced off the ionosphere. When I finished my thought, I had to say "over" to signal the HAM operator to release the transmission key and let Nancy talk and then she'd finish her thought, too, by saying "over."

As you can imagine lengthy, meaningful discussions were awkward at best and usually went something like this: Don: "Nancy, I love you, over." Frequently her response was indecipherable, and often the radio operator would help: "She says she loves you too, over." Still worse we were separated by about 12 time zones, so I had to call in the middle of the night to get her at a reasonable time the previous day. After several attempts to be heard by yelling "I love you, over" into the mouthpiece, the guys in the room next to the phone would respond, "She loves you too, now go back to bed so we can get some sleep."

On that particular evening, I doubted I'd be able to call again until after Christmas, so I closed by saying, "Merry Christmas. Tell the kids I love them too, over." When I finished saying this, the line at the other end was dead and I could only hope Nancy had heard. I hung up in despair, feeling isolated, uncertain and out of place in an unfamiliar, foreign and dangerous environment.

As I reflected on this unpleasant experience, I realized that my worst Christmas was similar, in some respects, to Mary and Joseph's first Christmas. They, too, were away from their home in Nazareth. Yet but a teenager, Mary had her first child far away from her mother and father and the support of friends and relatives. The comforts of home were nowhere to be found in the squalor of the stable. After the initial excitement of Jesus' birth and the visit of the shepherds and wise men, Mary and Joseph had to flee for their lives to an unfamiliar and foreign country. After my experience in Vietnam, I can better appreciate how they must have felt. I also know that my worst Christmas has helped me more fully appreciate being together with friends and family each Christmas since then.

To them and all of you I would say: "Merry Christmas. I love you, over."

Who said eight hours of sleep is "normal?"

I kid you not, as I write these words it's 5:08 a.m. and I have been up for two hours. My sleeplessness was prompt by a phone call from my health care provider the day before. It was one of those "robocalls," sent out to provide seemingly worthwhile information, when the real motive is to sell you something. The message from my health care provider warned me that 25% of Americans don't get enough sleep. Who can sleep after receiving that alarming information?

I was reminded of Acts 20:9 "Seated in a window was a young man named Eutychus, who was sinking into a deep sleep as Paul talked on and on. When he was sound asleep, he fell to the ground from the third story and was picked up dead."

Poor Eutychus. He probably failed to get a full night's sleep the night before. Either that or Paul was an extremely boring preacher. I can relate to Eutychus' situation because I often fail to get the "required" amount of sleep. In addition to the "robocall," the Fox News Channel had aired a program on insomnia and warned of dire consequences, perhaps national disaster, unless we all don't start getting more shuteye immediately. I was so worried after viewing that program that I tossed and turned for hours worrying about not getting enough sleep.

Some years ago, *USA Today* published a story in which they took an in-depth look at insomnia. I yawned as I read the story, which reported that Americans are spending less and less time in bed.

The day afterward a *Courier Journal* headline read: "Poll finds Americans getting too little sleep." The article reported that 40% of Americans say they have trouble staying awake on the job. James Walsh of the National Sleep Foundation (NSF) warned that there is an epidemic of sleepiness in our society. Are you kidding me? You mean we have a National Foundation for sleep? My 7:45 a.m. weekend group that I teach doesn't need an organization to help them sleep, they have me.

What's the sudden obsession with insomnia? You may have slept through this, but the first week in March was National Sleep Awareness week. This may come as a surprise to the NSF, but I am aware of sleep 365 days a year and I actually sleep a whole lot better when I'm not terrorized by front page headlines warning us of the dire consequences of not getting enough sleep.

I tell you what I've often wondered. Who established that we need eight hours of sleep? I have never, day in and day out, or maybe I should say night in and night out, gotten eight hours of sleep. When I was younger my normal shuteye was seven hours. Now, in my sixties I'm down to about 5.5 a night and often up and at 'em after about four hours. I think the people who stipulate eight hours are the same people who develop those ideal weight tables. These tables suggest that I should weigh in at about 143 pounds, a weight I haven't seen since Bobby Lewis was singing "I couldn't sleep at all last night" in the early '60s.

But who says eight hours is the standard? To get to the bottom of this, I conducted a survey at work a while back.

I sent out an email asking everyone how many hours they normally slept at night. I got 118 responses and the results confirmed my suspicions. The average minister at Southeast sleeps seven hours...and then he goes home. Just kidding.

According to the results of my informal survey, only 19% sleep eight hours or more a night. Women and staff members under the age of 50 slept a little more on balance. My conclusion is that the normal night's sleep of eight hours is not normal at all, but closer to seven hours. If eight hours is the norm, my sleep deficit accumulated over the past 6.5 decades is at least 25,725 hours.

On Friday evening during National Sleep Awareness Week, ABC's Barbara Walters was interviewing a sleep expert. Nancy had to wake me up from my stupor in the lazy boy to see the show. The expert decried the epidemic of sleeplessness in America and prescribed afternoon naps noting that many companies are providing time and facilities for employees to take "power naps." Southeast already has such a facility. It's called the sanctuary.

The Bible has a good deal to say about sleep, mentioning it 73 times. I like the Biblical reference to sleep that was paraphrased and posted over the nursery at a church somewhere. It read: "They shall not all sleep, but they will all be changed." 1 Corinthians 15:51 I have reduced these Biblical references to several basic principles.

1. Don't be anxious about anything. Turn your cares and concerns over to God, and you won't have any trouble sleeping. Proverbs 3:24, Philippians 4:6. Don't count sheep, count blessings.

2. You can sleep too much and miss opportunities to serve God. Proverbs 6:9; 20:13

3. God provides for our rest as well as everything else. Psalms 3:5; 4:8

It all comes back to trusting God to provide whatever we need. In Eutychus' case, he dozed off and fell out the window. Paul revived him and then they stayed up all night eating and talking and "The people took the young man home alive and were greatly comforted," even though they didn't get their recommended eight hours of sleep.

There's gold in them thar hills... or at least some glittering rocks (in my head)

Spring vacation this year was costly. We joined our kids in Blue Ridge, Georgia at a lovely cabin where I planned to lay around and nap, read past issues of AARP magazine, and watch reruns of the India-Pakistan cricket finals.

My daughter-in-law Rae, ever the creative one, had other plans. "Grumpa, guess what we're going to do?" said my granddaughter Amy. Without allowing me time to guess, she told me we were going to go panning for gems. I didn't know what this would entail but as the first girl born into the family in 80 years, "Whatever Lola (Amy) wants, Lola gets."

This expedition involved a two-hour drive into a very remote part of North Carolina. As we navigated the two lane roads, I saw civilization disappear in the rearview mirror and around each twist and turn of the narrow road I had visions of the movie "Deliverance."

Eventually we turned into the Ruby and Sapphire mine. We were the only customers and Grumpa, as is my custom, agreed to pay, thinking there would be a nominal entry fee.

I mean this was hardly Kings Dominion or Disney World. It cost one hundred and thirty five dollars. I swallowed hard, but there was no turning back now. I had promised the grand-kids...or more accurately their parents had promised them.

Charlie, a friendly guy whose smile revealed only a few teeth, met us and described the panning process. He had been in this line of work for 37 years, and he handed me a wood framed screen with a narrow wire mesh, two large buckets and a dirty pill container to hold my find. I got an empty Tylenol container, which I later found apropos due to the headache I was about to experience.

There were four 25-foot long water troughs called "flumes" through which dirty water was pumped to create a stream of sorts. We would use the rush of water to wash away the dirt from the multitude of gems. Charlie explained that the gems were in the dirt on the other side of the creek, and all we had to do was fill our buckets full of dirt, carry them back across the creek and begin panning.

I began washing away the dirt, dreaming of dozens of large sapphires and rubies. I'd give some to Nancy, the girls on the New Member team, my mom and still have enough left over to contemplate an early retirement. Actually at 65+ I may have missed the window for a legitimate early retire-ment, but you know what I mean.

I washed and washed. The dirt was carried away down-stream leaving dozens of what appeared to be gemlike rocks in my screen. Some glittered, some glistened. I summoned Charlie who would judge my find. He wore coke bottle glasses and leaned over my collection of stones, rearranging my pebbles and rubbing each one with a serious look on his face. Rather than the great news I anticipated, he said simply, "Nothing but rocks." I was crestfallen, then indignant. "You mean rocks, like the rocks I have in my head for paying $135 to clean dirt?"

I went through this process what seemed like 37 times before I heard Charlie say "You got one." I thought he was talking about a rather large rock the size of my thumb. Rather he carefully extracted a gem, about the size of a grain of sand and held it up to my eyes. "Congratulations," he said "that's a fine sapphire." I strained to see what he was referring to. "That's it?" I questioned. That was it.

I reached for the dirty Tylenol container I had been issued, not to hold my microscopic gem but hoping there was an aspirin or two for me to take for the headache I was getting.

My experience panning for gems got me thinking about my own spiritual journey. It seems like I spend a lot of time sorting through the mundane, the ordinary, the "dirt" in my day-to-day life searching for something of value. I devote enormous resources to live out the American dream. My focus is often on stuff that doesn't really matter in the eternal scheme of things---politics, sports, fiction, TV, my portfolio, etc., and I often glom on to something that glitters or sparkles only to discover that it fails to satisfy or fulfill---it's nothing but rocks.

The real gem for us, the only thing that provides lasting hope and value in our lives, and for eternity is Jesus and our relationship to him.

Matthew 13:44 "The kingdom of heaven is like treasure hidden in a field. When a man found it, he hid it again, and then in his joy went and sold all he had and bought that field.45 Again, the kingdom of heaven is like a merchant looking for fine pearls. 46 When he found one of great value, he went away and sold everything he had and bought it."

Remodeling our "croak" house

W hen Nancy and I turned into our subdivision following a weeklong stay with my mom, I fully expected to see a bus parked in front of our condo and "Extreme Makeover" host Ty Pennington poised to announce, "Move that bus!" The event that triggered my fantasy was my wife's latest project, remodeling our 13-year old condo. We had spent several days living with my mom while the project was finalized.

Now, I was on record as opposing the project for a number of reasons.

First, it was totally unnecessary. I mean we had only lived in the house for 13 years, and painting was so unnecessary, mostly because off-white is my favorite color, and it was only turning yellow in a few places. Another unnecessary expenditure was replacing our ceiling fans, which, by the way, we seldom used. "But it will increase the resale value of our house," Nancy countered. I summoned all the patience I was capable of (which I have been told is not a lot) and responded with exasperation, "Nancy, this is our 'croak' house. Our next move is to the funeral home. The resale value of our house is the kid's problem."

Second, the upgrades were really expensive. I love my wife. She is easy to get along with, and low maintenance for the most part. But when she partners with my good friend Brenda Schuele, who flips houses professionally, Nancy becomes a one woman economic recovery package that dwarfs a federal government bailout program.

I thought Nancy and I had an agreement on how much to spend. It seemed to me $499 would be more than enough. A little paint here, a new light fixture there and our place would look like new. As I watched the project evolve, however, the cost increased dramatically. In view of all the cost overruns, I had flash backs to my days at the Pentagon and those infamous excesses---$500 hammers and $600 toilet seats.

The toilet example is almost literally true. Midway in the project, I walked into the garage, which looked for all the world like a well stocked Home Depot warehouse full of remodeling supplies. Still in its box was a brand new toilet. "What on earth do we need a new toilet for?" I protested. Nancy's response was, I kid you not: "The old toilet was the wrong shade of white." The wrong shade of white?! You got to be kidding me! My 401K is in the toilet due to the economy, and now I'm spending my kid's inheritance replacing a toilet that is the improper shade of white.

Third, the redecorating was so untimely. Where projects in the Pentagon were rarely completed on time, ours was accelerated. It was originally planned for an August completion, which coincided with my trip to Korea. That made sense to me. However, the accelerated timeline pushed the project into a particularly busy period of time for me and, to be honest, I was aggravated when Nancy advised me on Friday evening that I had to clear the upstairs for painting before the weekend, which was only hours away.

I attacked the job with my usual energy and careless disregard for my personal safety, throwing books, papers and keepsakes into the upstairs closet. Unfortunately, before

I got to the stairs, I heard the top shelf in the closet come crashing down. "Somebody" had put too much stuff on the top shelf. I know I'm an ordained minister, practically a saint I am told, but while I suppressed any audible exclamation or expletive, I must confess that I sinned in my heart. Dirty frepersnatz, conshut, erbag!!

Now that we've moved back into our new and improved digs, I'm a little embarrassed at my whining and foot-dragging. Thanks to Brenda's expertise and hard work and Nancy's patience with me, our new interior really does look nice and was worth the minor inconveniences.

However, my reaction reminded me of some Christians I know. While billions of people don't know Jesus and morality in America is in a free fall, some of us can throw a hissy-fit at the most superficial changes or improvements around the church. I get this reoccurring picture of a line forming at the pearly gates as St. Peter listens to long time Christians complain about the pattern of the carpet in Heaven, the choir of angels singing too loudly and, worst of all, God isn't wearing a tie.

Here's the sobering reality: If you don't like change and new things, better not plan on going to heaven. The word "new" appears 192 times in the Bible and is particularly prominent in Revelation where John writes in chapter 21:1*ff* about seeing "a new heaven and a new earth, for the first heaven and the first earth had passed away, and there was no longer any sea. 2 I saw the Holy City, the new Jerusalem, coming down out of heaven from God, prepared as a bride beautifully dressed for her husband...5 He who was seated on the throne said, 'I am making everything new!'"

Nancy made everything new at our house and I appreciate the changes now. We are really enjoying our newly redecorated croak house while awaiting our new home in heaven. In the meantime, I'm kicking back in my new digs and enjoying a little bit of heaven on earth.

Fishing for men is far better than fishing for fish

I have never really liked fishing. I mean there is nothing about this activity that appeals to me. It's inconvenient. Usually you have to get up really early and go to some remote location unless you happen to have a well-stocked, 75-acre fishing lake in your backyard.

When you get to the lake there's all the equipment to tend to and the ever-present danger of tangled lines and fish-hooks stuck in your finger. Then there is the stinky aspect of fishing---slimy worms, decomposing minnows and fish guts. Oh yuck! Never mind the mosquitoes, West Nile virus and the opportunity to drown.

And where's the sport in outwitting an animal with an average IQ of 3. You see all those pictures of fisherman proudly displaying a string of mullets or a 30-pound carp and you wonder how difficult that must have been with a $175 graphite and titanium rod and reel, Global Precision Navigation gear, sonar fish finder and 200-horse power bass boat. I'm sure the dim-witted fish are in awe of us Homo Sapiens and our resourcefulness.

But what's the point. There are, in my opinion, three unpleasant and totally unrewarding outcomes when you go fishing. First, the one I experience most frequently is you go through the ordeal to get your line in the water and you catch nothing. Of all the mindless activities known to man, staring at a bobber for hours on end, waiting expectantly for even the hint of movement ranks right up there with viewing snooker on ESPN, conjugating Greek words, or watching "Dukes of Hazard" reruns.

The second unrewarding outcome is that you catch a fish but end up throwing it back. I'm a little fuzzy on this type of fishing. Presumably the fish is comfortable in his environment before I enticed him to bite into this barbed hook. I know I was pretty content before I had to grab this slimy, squirming, barbed Pisces and try to dehook him so I can throw him back to where he was before. What the point of that?

The third option is the most unpleasant of all. You keep the fish you catch, take it home, cut it open, rip its guts out, descale it, put the entrails in your neighbor's garbage on a hot August day, then cook and eat your catch. I love to eat fish, but buying it at the store is neater and far less expensive and time consuming.

Even though I don't enjoy fishing, I seem to be surrounded by fishermen. My dad fished, so did my uncles, my oldest son, and many people I admire including long time friend, Bob Dabney. All are inveterate fishermen. Once a year I go fishing with Bob at his invitation. Even though I'm not fond of fishing I do enjoy Bob's company so I dutifully purchase a one-day fishing license and head off to the fishing hole with Bob.

Now, fishing with Bob is as good as it gets. First, I always catch fish. Second, he makes it really easy. He has all the equipment; he baits my hook, and tells me where to throw my line. "There's a big one out there," he frequently says and often he's right. Occasionally, he tells me when to pull on the line to set the hook. Bob can make me a good fisherman despite my ineptitude.

After a recently completed annual fishing outing with Bob, I was reading Matthew 4:18-20 where Jesus calls his disciples and promises to make them "fishers of men." I was reminded of the similarities between fishing for fish and fishing for men. Fishing for men, like fishing for fish, has its downside. It's time consuming, takes a lot of patience and can put you in some uncomfortable positions. But it is a challenging activity that can be very rewarding and one that has eternal consequences.

As I researched fishers of men in the Bible, I observed that there are basically two types of spiritual fishing.

1. In Jesus' time, commercial fishermen usually used a net, and he mentioned that practice most often in his illustrations. For instance, when Jesus called his disciples they were casting their nets for fish. They put down their nets and followed him. I would liken spiritual fishing with a net to what the church does in the sanctuary. Large groups are brought in where they hear the Gospel message, many are "caught," give their lives to Christ and are saved. Other large events, such as the Easter pageant, are similar to fishing with nets.

2. The second type of spiritual fishing is with a hook and line or one to one, personal evangelism. Biblical examples are Philip and the Ethiopian eunuch in Acts chapter 8 and Jesus with the Samaritan woman at the well. In both cases bait was used to attract the "fish." "Do you understand what you are reading?" Philip asked. Jesus lured the Samaritan woman into a spiritual conversation by making a provocative statement. John 4:10 "Jesus answered her, 'If you knew the gift of God and who it is that asks you for a drink, you would have asked him and he would have given you living water.'" After the Ethiopian and Samaritan were hooked both "fish" heard the Gospel message.

What kind of fishing do you like the best? Christ has called us to be fishers of men. Had any bites lately?

Teaching English as an evangelistic exercise

Ephesians 3:23 "And whatever you do, do it heartily, as to the Lord and not to men, [24]knowing that from the Lord you will receive the reward of the inheritance; for you serve the Lord Christ."

I had completed teaching my first class at a local Christian university. The subject was English 101, and I was reading my "end of course" critiques.

As I studied my students' assessment of my performance, I was satisfied that I had gotten pretty good reviews, but apparently the class felt I graded too hard. One young woman wrote the following words, which are printed exactly as written: "Mr. Waddell grades to (sic) hard. He is a profectionist. (sic)" After reading the feedback, I just shook my head. I was a failure, and I wondered if I should teach again.

How I came to teach English is a complicated story, which had its origins at the University of Louisville in 1966. The story began at dinner one evening when my dad "advised" me that if I were going to graduate, I needed to declare a major area of study.

"Good point, Dad," I thought hoping this would not interfere with my social life or quest to become a life master at contract bridge. I had begun college as a premed student but soon discovered that was way too hard for me. They wanted me to memorize all sorts of bones, muscles and body parts with Latin names. So, I postponed making a final decision on my major well into my junior year when my dad forced my hand (and I don't mean my bridge hand), and said he wasn't going to pay my tuition unless I declared a major soon.

Being a practical sort of guy, I counted up all my class credits and to my surprise I had more English courses than math or science; and soon thereafter declared myself an English major without considering what on earth I would do with such a degree. I was subsequently accepted into Law School after graduation hoping to apply my writing skills as an attorney, but got drafted into the military and ended up as a fighter pilot, dropping bombs in a grammatically correct manner.

Since then I have found myself posing as a writer on many occasions. So as I considered what I might do when I retired from Southeast, my good friend, John Moore, suggested I start teaching at a local Christian university. I dreamed of teaching leadership, management, "Contract Bridge for fun and profit" or anything but English 101. But that's what they offered, and that's what I agreed to teach.

It wasn't as much fun as I hoped. Basically, the kids didn't have a great deal of interest in learning English...kind of like me when I was their age. Not to my surprise, my students weren't all that thrilled about conjugating verbs, identifying split infinitives and eliminating dangling participles.

While I felt an obligation to teach, my heart just wasn't in it, particularly after reading the end of course critiques and coming face to face with the reality that my students didn't really care about learning what I was teaching. This was a sobering realization since all my previous instructional experience at church, in the military and elsewhere had been teaching folks who at least acted like they wanted to learn. I'll set aside the class members who fall asleep in my weekend group since we do meet at 7:45 a.m. (The really righteous Christians come to church before 8:00. Just kidding.) I don't mind the slumbering Christians; it's just that the snoring is so disruptive.

I was expressing my misgivings to my friends at our monthly bridge group. (Unfortunately, they would tell you I'm still far from becoming a life master.) I told them how unappreciative my students were, but I also shared with them an email I had recently received from one of my students. Her email actually thanked me for teaching, and she cited several specific lessons she would take with her into her professional life. That was encouraging. Then she closed by saying: "I also want to thank you for sharing your faith during our class time. You have influenced me to become a Christian."

When I shared that with my good friend, self-appointed spiritual advisor and bridge partner Jim Whitworth, he put things in proper perspective when he reminded me that maybe I wasn't teaching to meet some personal need or even to sustain my wife's extravagant life style. Maybe God had me right where He wanted me to be, so I could share His truth with this young woman.

If you're like I am, you may get in the habit of looking at what you are doing from your own point of view. If a particular task is unpleasant or unrewarding, there is always a temptation to avoid it or let it go. My experience teaching has reminded me that God can use us in any situation, especially if we focus more on Him, and less on our objectives and our enjoyment. We can be used by Him, even when we're not being appreciated or having fun.

Maybe as an English 101 teacher, I wasn't such a failure after all, at least in the eternal scheme of things.

Would you choose your pet over your partner?

Recently, I was reading an article entitled "Would You Choose Your Pet Over Your Partner?" The article reported that "A new AP-Petside poll found that, when forced to choose, as many as 14 percent of current pet owners would tell their spouses or significant others to hit the road rather than ditch their pets."

I wondered what Nancy's response would be, so I asked her the same question. "Can you give me a while to think about that?" she responded without a hint of sarcasm. Hoping to sway my wife of 43 years, I reminded her of the last vet bill we received, $363. "That's a lot of money for a dog who contributes nothing materially to our household." Nancy reminded me of my last medical bill for an extended stay in the hospital. I had to admit she had a point.

Zac has lived with us for almost 11 years now, long enough for Nancy to get attached to the little booger. I remember when we first decided to get a dog. There was immediate disagreement here. I wanted a man's dog---maybe a Pit Bull or Doberman Pinscher to guard the house and keep us safe or a boxer I could rough house with. I came to my senses and realized that inevitably we would get a lap dog, probably a little yappy creature that would serve no useful purpose.

Nancy, who invariably gets her way in these sorts of discussions, wanted a Bichon Frise. "A what?" I asked. Nancy handed me a book with a picture of a Bichon on the cover. Honest to goodness it looked like an overgrown, curly-haired, rat with a Little Orphan Annie hairdo. This is clearly not a man's dog. "But it's so cute," Nancy said, taking about seven seconds to pronounce the word "cute."

As you can imagine a ritzy, aristocratic, pure breed, pampered dog like a Bichon Frise has a delicate digestive system that is easily upset. Zac pukes regularly if we fail to accommodate his dietary idiosyncrasies. Recently, the manufacturer of Zac's special "dietary" dog food changed the formula adding liver to the mix, and Zac's stomach rebelled at the "new and improved formula."

He began to throw up regularly, usually on our family heirlooms and priceless Persian rug. We called the vet and she agreed that the new concoction was not being well received by other owners of pampered, spoiled, over-priced mutts and suggested we try another brand. Unfortunately, the new brand has a mushy texture and is difficult to spoon into Zac's dish.

Sometime after the new food arrived, I went to the refrigerator looking for his new dog food. I didn't see the can I was looking for but noticed a plastic container containing what looked to be the new dog food. Nancy and I both have a good amount of melancholy temperament in us, so we prided ourselves in dividing Zac's food up meticulously into eight equal sections. I wasn't surprised, then, that Nancy had cleverly taken the soft, squishy food out of the can and put it in the plastic container so we could just scoop out the requisite amount. I measured out the exact amount and as is his custom, Zac gobbled it down enthusiastically.

Later that morning when Nancy got up, she asked if I had fed Zac. "Of course," I responded, "can't you tell by looking?" Zac was the picture of contentment, sleeping on his back on the sofa with his legs pointing skyward.

Some time later Nancy looked in the refrigerator and asked "What did you feed him; I don't see a can of dog food?" "I fed him the dog food you put in the blue plastic container." A look of condescension swept over her face; it was a look of disbelief and condemnation. "Donald," she said sounding very much like my mom addressing me when I was six. "That's not Zac's dog food...that's the refried beans left over from our nachos last night."

Zac may have had trouble with the new, "improved" dog food formula, but he had no problem with a generous helping of refried beans. I looked over at Zac, and I swore I saw a smile spread across his face. I remembered then a similar looking facial expression on our kids' faces when they were infants, just as they were about to pass gas...There was a pungent aroma in the den where he napped. I guess he was taking a siesta.

Fortunately, as Christians we don't have to choose between our pet and our spouse, but we do have to choose and these choices have serious, eternal consequences: Choices to affirm our faith, or deny it; choices to live out Godly lives or choose to live in sin. As the Israelites entered the Promised Land they had to make similar choices: To be loyal to the God who had delivered them from slavery or to sell out to the god of their adversaries.

Joshua 24:15 "But if serving the LORD seems undesirable to you, then choose for yourselves this day whom you will serve, whether the gods your forefathers served beyond the River, or the gods of the Amorites, in whose land you are living. But as for me and my household, we will serve the LORD."

How's your spiritual diet?

D espite my efforts to eat a balanced diet, I'd admit that I occasionally eat too much "unhealthy food." I know I shouldn't, but I work at a church with the ever-present temptation of left over donuts, cakes, casseroles and communions wafers.

If I weren't feeling guilty enough about this already, however, we have various watchdog groups to lecture us about our eating habits. I'm sure you've heard these self-appointed, health food nuts affectionately known as the "food police." When you listen to one of their press conferences you'd swear we're all going to die tomorrow. They seem determined to scare the health out of you.

Having previously condemned Mexican food, Chinese food and movie theater popcorn as tantamount to physician-assisted suicide, one of the "food police" groups then informed us that the standard American breakfast of eggs, bacon, toast and pancakes will send you to an early grave faster than you can say, "Jack Sprat could eat no fat." For my part, when I heard the announcement I immediately made an appointment with my attorney to ensure my will was in good order and subsequently ordered a cemetery plot...extra-large to accommodate the additional bulk I was sure to gain eating the standard American breakfast.

What really bothers me is that these self-appointed guardians of our diet serve up their findings with generous portions of overstatement, hyperbole and hysteria. One called a "Denny's Grand Slam" breakfast "death on a plate;" another referred to eggs as "death pills." If my grandmother had only known how deadly the breakfast was that she ate every day for 89 years, she would have died much sooner scared witless by the "food police."

I can remember my parents forcing me to eat lima beans and Brussels sprouts in the name of good health. When that didn't properly motivate me, they shamed me with images of starving Chinese children. "Think of all the starving children in China" they admonished as if I would just eat that last morsel of broccoli, millions of malnourished Chinese refugees would suddenly be healthy again. As a result, I grew up hating the Chinese. Now we're warned that everyone who eats Chinese food may die from heart disease or high blood pressure...serves them right for making me eat all those yucky vegetables.

Now I'm no nutritional expert, but I do believe that a balanced diet low in fat, salt and sugar is a good idea. I also think food is given to us by God to be enjoyed in moderation and without hysterical claims about imminent death with the next ice cream cone, Denny's breakfast or Sunday School donut.

Good nutrition's not that complicated really. There are three general categories of things we take into our bodies: poisons, things that will kill you or make you very sick; junk food, tasty and OK in moderation; and nutritional food, what we should eat to grow healthy bodies and live a long and productive life. Eat none of the first category, moderate amounts of the second and lots of the third. It's simple.

Now to more important matters...how's your spiritual diet? As I reflected on what we take into our bodies in terms of food, it occurred to me that there are direct parallels between our physical diet and our spiritual diet. We can take in spiritual poisons, junk food or nutritious food. Spiritual poisons include pornography, gossip, and heretical literature. Few of these things kill us outright. Rather they are like lead or mercury poisoning, which builds up over time until the individual becomes ill.

Likewise, there's ample spiritual junk food too, stuff we can read or watch and enjoy but doesn't contribute to knowing God any better. This stuff includes most TV, sports, novels, movies, etc. Absolutely nothing wrong with these endeavors, if consumed in moderation. However, if we spend too much time parked in front of the TV set, curled up in a chair reading a mindless novel or involved in recreation, our souls will atrophy spiritually.

But most importantly, we need to have a solid spiritual diet that consists of good, nutritious spiritual food. We need to frequent God's house to worship, learn and fellowship with other believers. Clearly the best source of this balanced diet is the Bible. Everything you need to grow a healthy spiritual body is right there, and we need to partake of this spiritual food often. We wouldn't go days without eating three square meals, and we shouldn't neglect our spiritual sustenance in the form of daily devotions, Bible studies, and meditating on God's word.

Maybe we should form our own watchdog group, the Center for a Balanced Spiritual Diet and try to scare the wits out of sinners. On second thought, Christ made it quite clear that we needn't be overly concerned about what we eat. In His words, "So do not worry, saying, 'What shall we eat?' or 'What shall we drink?' or 'What shall we wear?'...But seek first his kingdom and his righteousness, and all these things will be given to you as well." Matthew 6:31-33

That's the second unmanly thing you've done

As many of you know, Zac, our 10-year-old Bichon Frise is one of the original lap dogs, a wimpy, yappy, over-bred, high maintenance canine. Many dogs are bred to perform practical tasks such as sheep dogs, St. Bernard rescue dogs, drug/bomb sniffing dogs or even hunting dogs. Bichons are bred to be cute. That's it. Nothing practical. Nothing to brag about when guys get together after hunting or a ball game. He is just cute.

It was a Saturday afternoon in December. Zac was laying by my side, and I was watching a mindless bowl game featuring two mediocre teams that couldn't beat Seneca High School two out of three times. It was so bad I was looking forward to the commercial break hoping to glean a little entertainment before I had to go to church for services.

As I sat in front of the TV in a semi-catatonic state, almost on cue, a Miller Lite commercial came on. You probably remember this one. A group of guys are slamming down Miller Lites and one guy taunts a buddy who opted for a normal beer saying "That's the second unmanly thing you've done today." "What was the first?" is the response. Then depending on which version you are watching, we learn that the uncool guy was seen riding a scooter with elderly women, freaks out when wall climbing, or panics when landing a slimy fish.

Of all the unmanly members of the male gender, Zac is the least masculine. After neutering, he barely qualifies as a man. He is an embarrassment to his species, his gender and my good name. (I cringe every time the receptionist as the Vet's office refers to him as "Zac Waddell.") Here are some of the unmanly things he does.

1) Zac hates to get wet, which creates a problem when it's raining outside or when I have to give him a bath. When it's raining I have to literally drag him outside to do his stuff as I did that Saturday in December. I don't know who was the least manly; Zac afraid of a little rain or me holding a dad gum umbrella over him while he pees?? It was a ridiculous sight.

2) When he realizes it's bath time, the coward becomes a quivering mass of pusillanimous protoplasm and tries to hide under Nancy's shoes in the closet.

3) He barks jealously and loudly when Nancy and I hug. If he were a real man, he'd bite me or something.

Zac is exceedingly unmanly, but if I am totally honest, I'd admit that as a Christian husband and dad I've done some unmanly things myself. The Bible sets a pretty high standard for men as the spiritual head of the house, but I have often fallen short.

Ephesians 6:4 says: "And you, fathers, do not provoke your children to wrath, but bring them up in the training and admonition of the Lord." I get the part about not provoking your children, particularly as they became teenagers and were bigger and stronger than I was. The part I struggled with was "bringing them up in the training and admonition of the Lord."

As the head of the household (Ephesians 5:22-24; 1 Cor. 11:3), it is the dad's responsibility to teach their kids about the Lord and instruct them how to live as a Christian in an unchristian world. He should model a life of service, Bible study and prayer.

While I did a really good job of taking my kids to church, I didn't do as well promoting their faith by modeling my Christian walk in praying with them, reading the Bible to them and participating with them in church activities. Like many men, my wife, Nancy was the more spiritually mature, and I acquiesced to her initiative. Bad on me.

That's why I am pleased that our church has made a major commitment to elevating the role of men in their families and in the church. A portion of our mission, vision, strategy reads: "Building spiritually healthy homes by equipping Godly men to lead and pray for their family." I expect God will bless us as we seek to conform more closely to His will in this regard.

I returned home from church later that Saturday. I had recorded the UL-Memphis basketball game and managed to get home without learning the outcome. I stepped boldly into the den and announced I was ready to watch the game. Nancy could do whatever she wanted, but the man of the house was home, the king of the castle had arrived. It was time to watch some basketball.

Unfortunately for me, my daughter Dawn had dropped by for a visit and she and Nancy were watching some chick flick on the very TV my DVR was hooked up to. "But I want to watch the game," I whined. Nancy put her finger to her lips suggesting I sit down and be quiet. "We'll be done in two hours," she announced.

My shoulders slumped in disappointment; my morale was crushed. I turned to leave the room when my eyes met Zac's. I swear he winked and looked at me with a mixture of contempt, sympathy and condescension as if to say, "That's the second unmanly thing you've done today."

Were there toys in the manger on Christmas Day?

E very Christmas Nancy and I make our annual winter
pilgrimage to Tallahassee to spend Christmas with our
two sons and their families. A key attraction is the opportunity to spoil our grandchildren Donnie, Devin, Amy and
Erin.

Invariably I am involved with toys during this visit either
in buying, assembling, or the subsequent repair. Each activity
can be a bit frustrating, but grandfathers have their role to
play even if it's not as glamorous as grandma's. This year's
contest between granddad and the toy manufactures of the
world was particularly noteworthy and in today's column I'd
like to describe my experience. See if you can relate to it.

First, I don't think I assembled or wrapped one toy this
year that wasn't made in China. Seriously. As far as I could
determine these toys were made as well as any others, but
there were a few exasperating details designed to confound
granddads called into action on Christmas Eve just after
midnight.

Problem one: Each package contained those three dreaded
words no man wants to read just after the clock strikes 12 on
Christmas eve: "Some assembly required." Sure enough I

was assigned the task of assembling the "Made in China" scooter. I read on the carton the tools required for assembly---screwdriver, pliers and a six-way spanner wrench. A spanner wrench??

There probably aren't two households in American that have a spanner wrench. I search diligently for a spanner wrench first in the carton and then in my son's tool chest, which unfortunately was no better organized than mine. Eventually, the scooter was assembled with the brakes hand tightened. In fact, this didn't turn out to be a problem, because it was too cold to ride that Christmas and Donnie fell in love with a cheaper toy.

Problem two. While our Oriental entrepreneurs have managed to manufacture reasonable toys, they haven't perfected the fine art of writing instructions just yet. These narratives are indecipherable by the average granddad when he's fully alert, never mind several hours after his normal bedtime.

One example was contained in the instructions for a 35mm camera. Now perhaps we shouldn't expect too much from a camera that costs $7.99. The instructions began (this is precisely how they were written): "Dear Customer: Thank you for buying our 35mm camera Allow me to explain something to you: How the 35mm camera works well? When you pull out the rewinder knob. Please don't pull it out too hard. May be you can find a experienced person to help you. When you loaded the film it should be loaded in proper position (right on the gears). Then close the back tightly...When you can take a nice picture, this is a good timing from 8:00 AM till 11:00 Am and from 2:30 PM till 4:30 PM. The subject should have to face the enough sunshine then you can take a good picture...Sincerely Yours,"

As I typed the above instructions, my computer's spell/ grammar checker was overheating trying to make sense out of the spelling and syntax. In truth, I wasn't sure it was written by someone from China or my English 101 class, I wrote about earlier.

My favorite toy was a remotely controlled, dual motor Power'n Hit toy that would automatically hurl a plastic baseball for the child to hit. It was really nifty. The bat contained a button activated transmitter that, when depressed, caused a battery operated machine to release the ball which would be pitched to the batter. The instructions claimed that the toy contained "two aerodynamic curve balls that randomly pitched left or right curve balls, screw balls, slider and sinkers." For this the New York Yankees would pay $250 million dollars. We paid $29.95.

The toy really worked--too well if you ask me. I struck out the first three times I tried to hit the ball. I was a little chagrined when my four-year-old grandson, hit two out of three. Said Nancy gleefully: "You did better than granddad." Crestfallen, I limped back in the house to watch the second half of the Saniflush Holiday Bowl.

But that embarrassment paled in comparison to my feeling when my MS afflicted, non-athletic wife, Nancy, hit one over the house. To add insult to injury, it occurred to me that as a granddad I was no longer needed for pitch and catch. I had been replaced by a machine costing less than $30. My importance to my grandsons had been reduced to the person who changes the batteries.

As for Christmas day, we established some new records. I think all the presents for Donnie 5th and Devin were opened in seven and a half minutes, and the first child was crying in nine. I surveyed the scene that looked something similar to a combat zone, and noted several thousand dollars worth of toys scattered about. Ironically, our two year old was most deeply absorbed with a cheap, dollar and ninety-nine cent foam rubber airplane purchased as an after thought to fill a stocking. Go figure.

As our family gathered together that Christmas morning and read the Christmas story from Luke, it was reassuring to be reminded that the real message of Christmas has less to do with the gifts we give each other than it does the eternal gift God gave us on that first Christmas day over 2000 years ago. Isaiah 9:6 "For unto us a child is born, unto us a son is given: and the government shall be upon his shoulder: and his name shall be called Wonderful, Counselor, The mighty God, The everlasting Father, The Prince of Peace."

Valentine's Day shopping at Cracker Barrel can be very expensive

E very year it's the same thing. As the month of February approaches I am stuck with what to get my Valentine for Valentine's Day. Last year I had some luck at Cracker Barrel. Not every guy can get away with doing his Valentine's Day shopping at Cracker Barrel, but when I saw the gift it was love at first sight---a cute little chimp with a heart around its neck.

Due to a miracle of modern technology the chimp had a motion detector in its head and would whistle when it sensed motion in the area. I knew Nancy would be enthralled and placed it on the kitchen table where it would greet her first thing in the morning with its piercing whistle. She was surprised all right, but perhaps in not an altogether positive way. She was flattered, too, until she discovered that the chimp also whistled when the cat passed by. (I guess that's why it's called a "cat call.")

Undeterred by this temporary setback, I again returned to Cracker Barrel this year. I remembered that flowers are a girl's best friend, or maybe it's diamonds, I forget. So while replenishing my cholesterol reserves at Cracker Barrel, I noticed a singing potted plant for sale. It employed technology similar to that great technical innovation of the 20th Century, "the clapper" which turns lights on and off with the clap of one's hands. In this case, when you clap, the singing posy serenades you with a round of "Somewhere over the rainbow" while its eyes blink seductively. Though my intentions were good, I was "somewhere over the rainbow" when I told Nancy this was her Valentine's present.

The Greek word for sin is "hamartia" which means "to miss the mark." That being the case, I sinned. Being a Christian, Nancy was willing to forgive me...for a price. So, off we went to the jewelers, this time I was accompanied by my Valentine so I would get it right. Nancy wanted a cross and necklace and my head began to spin when I was confronted with the bewildering array of crosses available for purchase.

I saw a nice one for $19.95 which elicited a negative response from Nancy. "Oh that's gold filled," she said disapprovingly. Filled with gold didn't sound too bad to me, but the salesman directed us to another section of jewelry where the prices had more zeros on the end. I gasped when I saw the first one and was barely able to speak: "Do you have something in plastic?" I asked. Well, a solid gold cross now adorns my Valentine's neck, and I think she knows how much she means to me.

This problem buying gifts is a gender related problem. I ran into Burch Moberly in the Living Word the day before Valentine's Day some years ago. He was shopping for his Valentine and fiancée, O'Neal Briel. The next day in Sunday School, I mentioned to O'Neal that I had run into Burch in the Living Word, and she confessed that she had sent him there to buy a book or two to read on their honeymoon.

I was taken aback by this revelation. I don't remember taking any books on my honeymoon. Perhaps I was missing something here. I was really bewildered when I learned that the book she recommended he buy was "Left Behind." That's a curious thought to begin a honeymoon with. When I shared this story with Charlie Faust, he saw the humor in the situation and added that it's just a good thing O'Neal didn't recommend another book in the Left Behind series, "Tribulation Force."

On Valentine's Day, the *Courier Journal* printed a feature article entitled "What Is Love?" and consulted several Louisville psychologists to define love. You think I missed the mark with the singing posy, you should read the nonsense these "experts" offered. They spoke of "attachment theory" and "evolutionary psychology."

One psychologist said, "I think that falling in love is a biological process. There is the survival of the species to think about and that we are programmed to find somebody so that we can propagate." (I agree in so far as I was deeply concerned about my survival when I gave Nancy the singing posy.) Another psychologist referred to the "triangle" theory of love, which consists of three components---passion, commitment and intimacy.

I rather like the "triangle" theory a couple described in a Wednesday evening testimonial. Their triangle places Jesus at the apex of the triangle with the husband and wife at the bottom corners. The closer each one gets to Jesus, the closer they get to each other. If you really want to get closer to your mate, get closer to Jesus, the wellspring of love. In John 15:12 Jesus said: "My command is this: Love each other as I have loved you. Greater love has no one than this, that he lay down his life for his friends."

You won't be finding that kind of love at Cracker Barrel, the jewelers or any place apart from the cross. Not a gold cross either, but a wooden one, which held our Lord 2000 years ago.

DNR for the dog?

Though it was only 8 a.m. it had already been a traumatic day for our beloved 9-year-old Bichon Frise,
Zacchaeus. As we entered the veterinarian's office, Zac was
shaking noticeably and his tail was tucked between his legs.
Compounding his nervousness was the fact that he had been
fasting for 12 hours and had to take his morning walk on a
snowy February morning. As you can imagine when you're
only 15" tall (we're talking about Zac now, not me) squatting
in 8" of snow to perform your daily routine can be uncomfortable at best.

The reason we were at the vet when most normal people
are still in bed was that Zac was scheduled for his annual
checkup and quadrennial teeth cleaning. Now the teeth
cleaning thing was still a difficult concept to grasp. Growing
up my dogs did not go to the dentist. Nancy grew up on a
farm where the dogs seldom came indoors, never mind went
to the vet for a brighter smile and fresher breath.

The receptionist at the vet's was friendly and explained
all the options as Zac quivered nervously in the corner. As
a man and Zac's owner, I was embarrassed at what a wimp
he was, our pusillanimous canine quivered nervously in the
corner. Meanwhile, a sissified female French poodle pranced

in boldly while Zac was "quaking in his paws" (to coin a phrase), and I was embarrassed beyond belief. "You're an embarrassment to your gender," I scolded forgetting for a moment that an operation he had 8 years before had made his gender all but irrelevant.

As the friendly receptionist explained the options, all I could see were the dollar signs next to each choice. Seems to me we had already underwritten college tuition for our vet's two kids and paid for his country club membership. There was a charge for anesthesia, but couldn't we just give him a bullet to bite? Charge for sealant. Charge for postoperative care, kennel rental. "Isn't this covered under my health care plan," I asked hopefully. If there ever was an example of a dependent, Zac was it. All that was missing was the purple plastic toothbrush my dental hygienist gives me after each visit.

Now traumatized by the mounting bill, I was unable to focus on her words, but I think she asked about a living will and DNR. Not only did I have questions about DNR, but I was seriously considering changing the purpose of the vet visit from teeth cleaning to euthanasia, which I prefer to call allowing Zac to take a very long nap.

This incident reminded me of our previous dog Ebber who we adopted in 1981. He was the unfortunate victim of a divorce. My brother-in-law divorced his wife and in the settlement she said "no dogs." Then he remarried and his new wife said "no dogs." Suddenly Ebber was homeless and not eligible for government aid. Nancy and I were returning from a tour overseas and happened on the scene just in time to rescue Ebber from homelessness or worse.

Unbeknownst to us, Ebber came with a host of medical problems, which we began to treat. (I saw my lawyer about a truth in advertising lawsuit again my brother-in-law.) During the subsequent trips to the vet after Ebber had moved on to "doggie heaven," he advised us that Zac should have his teeth cleaned, and while he was anesthetized he may as well be neutered too. As a member of the masculine persuasion, I commiserated with Zac and considered the irony of this situation: clean teeth now but nothing to smile about.

Though he was a delightful dog, Ebber's travails continued and his health declined. Finally Nancy ordered me to take him to the vet to get the long awaited very long nap. I told her she should take him, reminding her that it was her brother who gave us the pet without disclosing the defective nature of the product.

She told me to quit whining and go to the vet. The young vet, who had recently graduated from Veterinarian School assured me, "I think I can save your dog" and gave him a shot of some miracle drug. My shy, retiring, soft spoken, gentle Nancy was outraged when she came home to find Ebber sleeping in his bed. I was clearly in the "dog house" now.

The miracle drug lasted until early the next day when Ebber passed away into doggie heaven. I buried him in the back yard following a brief but meaningful ceremony. Though Nancy was miffed, the good news was that the shot of the "miracle" drug cost less than the cost of putting Ebber to sleep.

We love our pets don't we? Inevitably when the subject comes up at church, the question is asked as to whether or not we will see our pets in Heaven. Former Southeast Senior Minister Bob Russell asserts that his pet, Bandit, isn't in Heaven, but rather in the other place. But those of us who have pets we love still wonder.

In his book, *Heaven*, Randy Alcorn suggests we might see our pets again. He argues that since we know there will be animals in Heaven (e.g. Rev. 5:13), it is logical to assume our pets may be there. For my part, I'm not sure I agree, since for Zac to make it to Heaven, he'd have to have a soul, and I'm not sure there's any Biblical support for that thesis. But with God all things are possible, Nancy reminds me.

Since the Bible is not clear on this issue, I recommend you believe that you will see your pet in Heaven (but not if its name is "Bandit"). If Zac ends up in Heaven, great; if not, the Bible promises I won't be disappointed ("no more sorrow"). And no more budget-busting vet bills either.

The issue is largely academic, and not essential to our faith. One thing I do know is that if Zac makes it to heaven, he'll now have a heavenly smile, and when we meet at the Pearly Gates, he'll be smiling broadly and displaying his pearly whites.

Dinners for Eight, minus
the hostess

⊨◇⊣

Some years ago I was speaking in Battle Creek, Michigan.
When I returned to the hotel room in the afternoon
I called Nancy just to check in. However the voice that
answered the phone was not a familiar one. "May I speak
to Nancy?" I asked. "Oh, she's not here. She left for Florida
this morning," responded the unfamiliar voice. "I'm the dog
sitter, can I take a message?" "No," I replied, "this is her
husband. Who are you?" I learned that the unfamiliar voice
was my nephew's wife, who had been recruited by Nancy to
watch Zac while I was out of town.

I was miffed. My wife left me without the decency of
telling me to my face. To be honest, I wasn't too surprised.
Our fourth grandchild, Amy Nicole Waddell had been born
recently, and Nancy was eager to get down to Tallahassee
and start spoiling Amy, the first girl born into the Waddell
family in 80 years.

Later that night I was in my hotel room deeply absorbed
in the Slippery Rock – Southwest Carolina football game
when Nancy called from Montgomery. "Sorry I just couldn't
wait for you to get back in town. Please don't hate me. Oh,

and by the way, don't forget that you have 'Dinners for 8' at our house this Friday."

I do recall discussing this possibility, but now the full impact of what I had agreed to hit me like a ton of leftover casseroles. The real crisis was that "Dinners for 8" had now become "Dinners for 7" (without Nancy), and I was going to have to do all the work. Cooking is not my spiritual gift; hospitality isn't a fruit of the spirit.

"Not to worry," Nancy intoned cavalierly, "the table is already set, the maid is coming twice next week and everyone knows what they are supposed to bring. Not even you could screw this up." "Want to bet?" I said under my breath and called my mother as soon as Nancy hung up.

I knew my mom could help me pull this off and would ensure that there were no awkward lapses in conversation. But now the event had become "Dinners for 9" and I wasn't sure our dining room table was even big enough. I returned home from Michigan and sure enough, Nancy had added a leaf to the table, put out seven settings of china and covered the whole table with a sheet to protect it from dust.

Now one of the reasons Nancy wanted to go ahead with the event was to show off her newly painted and wallpapered living area. One thing I have learned after 36 years of marriage is that when I ask Nancy how much something costs and she says, "You don't want to know," I really don't want to know. Once I made the mistake of pressing her for an answer, and I was so stunned I went into shock-induced depression for several months. Still, our place did look nice, and I was willing to show it off, even if Nancy was AWOL.

As the big day approached, I began to worry about all the details. If you're not familiar with the "Dinners for 8," there are a few ground rules you should know about. Generally, one couple brings a salad, one couple brings a vegetable and one brings the dessert. The host (that would be me and the dog in this case) provides a starch and the meat. I seriously

271

considered nine happy meals from McDonald's but ended up trundling off to our favorite chicken carry out restaurant.

This was a cop out, I know, but I respect my group too much to make them eat anything I would cook. While I waited for my order to be completed, I asked the owner if PETA was going to demonstrate at his restaurant like they had at other chicken outlets recently. "No," he replied "they don't have a bone to pick with us (a wish bone I presume), all our chickens are volunteers." I was greatly relieved to learn that.

The housecleaner did come twice that week and our house was in wonderful condition. Not even Zac and I could mess up a house too badly in one day. It was an eerie feeling as I tidied up before the arrival of my guests. Nancy was 675 miles away, well out of earshot, but I could distinctly hear her nagging me. "Remember to sweep the porch, honey," she said to me vicariously. "Take off your shoes...don't mess up the den...don't use the guest bath toilet before the guests arrive." I got so miffed during this imagined nagging that 10 minutes before our guest arrived I went in and used the toilet in the guest room...and left the seat up. "That'll teach her to harass me from 675 miles away."

Dinner and the subsequent merriment went very well despite my whining and foot-dragging. But in the final analysis, "Dinners for 8" are about more than fried chicken, baked beans and rich desserts. It's mostly about the body of Christ building eternal relationships, and it's actually a great model taken right out of the Bible in Acts 2:42: "They devoted themselves to the apostles' teaching and to the fellowship, to the breaking of bread and to prayer...46 Every day they continued to meet together in the temple courts. They broke bread in their homes and ate together with glad and sincere hearts, 47 praising God and enjoying the favor of all the people."

About the Author

The Waddell Clan. In case you are wondering,
I am the bald one.

D on came to Christ as a nine-year-old at South Louisville Christian Church and then moved with his parents in 1962 to help start Southeast Christian Church. After graduating from the University of Louisville and getting married in 1967, Don was drafted and spent 28 years in the Air Force as a fighter pilot and commander. When he retired in 1995, he returned to Southeast where he now serves as New Member Minister. He is married to the former Nancy Smith and they have three children (Don 4, David, and Dawn) and four grandchildren (Don 5, Devin, Erin and Amy).

CPSIA information can be obtained at www.ICGtesting.com
Printed in the USA
LVOW132046100512

281250LV00001B/2/P